SELECTED POEMS

SELECTED POEMS

MARK FORD

COFFEE HOUSE PRESS

2014

COPYRIGHT © 2014 by Mark Ford
COVER AND BOOK DESIGN by Linda Koutsky
COVER ART © Joe Brainard
AUTHOR PHOTOGRAPH © Mary Hinkley, UCL

COFFEE HOUSE PRESS books are available to the trade through our primary distributor, Consortium Book Sales & Distribution, cbsd.com or (800) 283-3572. For personal orders, catalogs, or other information, write to: info@coffeehousepress.org.

Coffee House Press is a nonprofit literary publishing house. Support from private foundations, corporate giving programs, government programs, and generous individuals helps make the publication of our books possible. We gratefully acknowledge their support in detail in the back of this book. To you and our many readers around the world, we send our thanks for your continuing support.

Visit us at coffeehousepress.org.

LIBRARY OF CONGRESS CIP INFORMATION
Ford, Mark, 1962 June 24–
[Poems. Selections]
Selected Poems / by Mark Ford.
pages cm
Includes bibliographical references.
ISBN 978-1-56689-349-7 (Paperback)
ISBN 978-1-56689-362-6 (Hardcover)
I. Title.
PR6106.074A6 2014
821'.92—DC23
2013035160
PRINTED IN CANADA
FIRST EDITION | FIRST PRINTING

Poems from *Soft Sift* (2001) and *Six Children* (2011) are reprinted by permission of Faber & Faber, Ltd. Copyright © 2001, 2011 by Mark Ford.

Poems from *Landlocked* (1992) were originally published by Chatto & Windus.

SELECTED POEMS

CONTENTS

FROM **SOFT SIFT** (2001)

FROM SIX CHILDREN (2011)

NEW POEMS

FROM

LANDLOCKED

1992

If You Could Only See Me Now!

When I'm in power I will pursue landlords
across the country. Right now, life
has me boxed in, and my cries for help drift inscrutably
around willows, oak trees, and grief-stricken elms.
I left home young, and since then I've roamed
and roamed, following my nose, through deserts and cities,
always alone, in forests, living in trees—
What a life!
                    They say every character is complex,
but I am tangled up like spaghetti; I lie here, observing the stars,
a stiffening breeze tickling my feet, my pillow
a petrified log. The birds chirruping in the early dawn
ignore me, while I dream I am a lunatic, striding the land,
scattering seed and crushing the asphodel
beneath my pitiless heel;
but finally the day arrives,
bursting softly over the horizon.
                              For the West
has been ruined. You left under a cloud
but I love you. If you could only see me
now! I stand here, incompetent,
tracing figures on a map, fully dressed
as if it were already evening, enraged
and impenitent, clenching my teeth.

I

Christmas

I very much enjoyed your latest book I lied having
NOT read it. Hurrah! We're all of us bright as chickens
As if Jack liked Chrissie and Chrissie liked Jack.
Ah, we had a good season, then, we drew all five fixtures!
For Christmas, I asked my mother to knit me a tie
To go with my tunic. "No!" she snapped,
"Go out and buy one." So off I samba—
When it was Sunday and all the shops were shut—
The streets are full enough though and there are
Some fine ankles showing through—my fertile imagination!—
I see miniskirts where others see only galoshes,
I can count all my exes at the bus stop
All over with tinsel, polluting the atmosphere with
Their dirty breaths. It is lunchtime
So I hail a friend munching a pastrami sandwich—
He spotted me and then he lay flat in the snow.
"Stop playing hookey," I yelled, "you're grown up now!"
Then I thought—but what if something is really wrong?
I screeched to a halt beside his head
The snow spooning up into my sandals, and I shouted
"Get up, Jake," and I toed him. Any moment
I expect him to grab me playfully by the ankle,
I quite liked the idea of a tussle in the Christmas snow
On Main Street. He didn't budge though.
Only the yellow stains of the mustard from his sandwich drooled
Scenting the crisp air. "Ah, come on Jake,
You think this a rodeo?" I whisper to him,
"Why not get up?" And I threaten him with

The police, arrest, his sister in tears on the phone.
And I poured hot coffee down his throat, murmuring
"But it's the season of goodwill, no one plays for keeps
Over Christmas." What kept him down there,
Face in the slush, people must've seen him eating
Pastrami sandwiches before?
                              Apparently not. I waited
All afternoon by him, chain-smoking his Camels,
And then I watched his feet disappear into the ambulance
That arrived after dark. I stamped his damp sandwich
Back into the snow. People, I thought,
Will find this when the thaw sets in
And wonder about it, shopping or on their way to work,
Birds like sparrows will nibble the sesame seeds
And wish it were pumpernickel,
It will liven up their Easter.

Landlocked

See, no hands! she cried
Sailing down the turnpike,
And flapped her arms like a pigeon,
And from the backseat Solomon, her spaniel, answered her
By woofing ever more madly at each passing car!
What a trek it was out west
And back again! Weeks on end she spent
Stranded in the worst motels, poor thing,
Could never quite make up her mind to go on
To go back, to stay absolutely where she was.
Such awful doubts assailed her in the prairie states—
For days she chewed her favorite gum on the hard shoulder
And whispered her difficult secrets to the wheat
Where game Solomon yelped, and, true to form,
The unmiraculous wheat only rustled through its rosary once more.
She sent me a postcard from somewhere
In Missouri, and then again from Amarillo,
Texas. She said she thought she'd make it
All the way to sunshine California, but she said
She couldn't promise she'd like it when she did
Or even that she'd get all the way over to the ocean there,
Which didn't surprise me or disappoint me one little bit,
And I sent one back to an address in Vegas saying,
Well why should you, unless of course you want to?

Street Violence

I asked for nothing better than a five-spot.
I thought that modest. Whisking around
On her single stiletto, though, her lips twitching,
She stared me in the eye so forcefully
I saw only the familiar words—
Nothing Doing. I determined there and then
To take each disappointment as best I could.
There you have it, once we were so close
Nothing short of a machete
Could have separated us. Now . . .
I watched her hail a shiny yellow taxi.
It was such a wonderful afternoon!
I moved off down the block, my block,
Its bright red bricks seemed to watch me,
There was a sudden breeze fresh in my face
And the sun was so strong it made my eyes water.
Too bad, I thought, for her sake,
That she didn't remember me like she should have.

General Knowledge

Atlanta emerged from the ribbed, red soil
Of Georgia; it now has
One of the busiest airports in America.

From there we flew to the cradling arms
Of New Orleans; here, where the Mississippi
Ends, perspiring jazz musicians like bulls lock horns.

It's said that every forty minutes the world is girdled
By a satellite; with a nail I trace the thin blue
Veins of the delta winding dubiously toward the sea.

Stocking Up

No one lives in the imagination, or if they do
they probably stink of garlic. What a thought!
Five o'clock. Everyone's pushing off to the country for the weekend.
What a jamboree the streets enjoy, sticky
traffic jams, spouting hydrants, and roofs that catch the red and dying sun.
While Tom Cat plays with baby, there's Mother
waving us farewell. "Drive carefully," she cries
as we pull out, "it's Friday night, remember."
We slide so easily though through strings of amber traffic lights
on our smooth journey to the shops, our windows rolled down
all the way. The light
lies down beautifully over the new arcade.
What a lovely evening! My trolley is overflowing
with supplies. In the low, flat sweep of store window
my friends and I see ourselves reflected.
The lot behind us is beginning to fill up,
could be they'll introduce valet parking at some point. Pleased,
we fill up the trunk and go back for more
("You again" the cash girl joked us),
enough to feed us and our families for
a part, at least, of the long, hot summer now approaching.

Invisible Assets

After he threw her through a
plate glass window, nature seemed that much closer.

Even the dastardly divisions in society
might be healed by a first-rate glazier.

Of course, on Sundays families still picnicked
boldly on the village green, and afterwards

marveled at the blacksmith's glowing forge—
how strong they all were in those days!

And yet how small! Even a man only six foot tall
was then esteemed a veritable giant.

Surely the current furor over architecture
would have evoked from them only pitying smiles.

Meanwhile, the market for landscapes has never
been firmer. This view, for instance, includes

seven counties, and a bull charging around in its paddock.

Daily

Newspaper clippings drift
across the Walworth Road,
and, in the unmentionable cold, the shops
incline their shutters. I imagine
chalk dinosaurs erupting from the doorways,
and a tinkle of glass to accompany
the carefree motion of their scaly tails . . .

Inside, the soup
has already congealed inside the single pan
around whose rim moss sprouts,
and released into the air the innumerable sightless microbes
that will later perplex the authorities.
Hungry pets yelp in locked attics, while we gawp
as at last the rubbish enters the furnace.
Turn out the light—some story
is breaking, crumbling, collapsing
under the intolerable weight of fresh evidence
whispered over telephones and hedges: awful
types prosper and suddenly the rhumba
is everywhere the rage again, a perfect dance
for couples or singles, for either in front
of the mirror or actually on the crowded dance floor.

Winter Underwear

How vividly the football flew
Only he would remember;
And likewise the dark purple scarves
In which the body was later wound.

Until one day speech
Is merely syntax, and one's head
Is so full of stratagems
The tea freezes solid in its pot;

And a fresh snow covers the plains
Above which newfangled aircraft constantly
Maneuver, their vapor trails soft
And brilliant as the white

Winter underwear she is even now pulling on.

I'm

I'm an aggressive man
Always walking up escalators
And sniffing out rights. Sharks
Infest our local waters,
You too I despise.
                     Night floods the land.
We must leave now. Armies of flowers
Advance, stealing the oxygen
Right out of our mouths.

Free the Spirit

So polite he could almost have been
The villain in a Charlotte Brontë novel—

If only he knew what we were about to do!
A school bell rings shrilly in the distance

And the very seconds prepare to choke
On their own significance, marked out by an orange kitchen clock.

Noon arrives nursing its own peculiar threats;
No wind and a soft meowing sound

Accompany the last hopes of the vanishing day, and soon
It will be more than late enough for a drink.

Leaving, on the other hand, would mean
Forking out for a new haircut, and arguing

The whole thing through with the face man again.

Snowfall

You must be snug in there
you and your seventh TV wife
with a cat and a fire, I swear
I'm so glad you ended up with that.

He writes! How wonderful. And
bloodies his own nails and nose
for sensation. He has a firm hand-
shake, why I'm glad of their liaison.

And she sweet vague snowdrop
is also carefully posed each morning. Does he
draw her? They sketch each other! And what could stop
her melting but amnesia?

I've a new taste in my mouth all day.
It rises overnight and hangs there,
and chokes my breath, all morning I say
this final straw, now chew it over . . . please.

My system! I fiddle while Rome burns. But find
another, or more untrampled snow
which doesn't exist. Kind kind
rain has pockmarked everything.

In the afternoon I swept
the porch and yard and dressed. We left
in the early evening, under gray skies, the car leapt
into life, and I relaxed with a sigh into its rich upholstery.

Hush! my mother said . . . The lights
are green but she won't go.
Move! Mother, I said, nights
are long on the Pulaski Skyway.

We shunt around town for hours.
Ah, Mother, she must have been held up,
her car wouldn't start! Even ours
is unsafe in this blizzard.

Oh Mother, I'm sorry. Let's go,
we'll go home. Don't say anything,
please, I wish we didn't know
each other so well, drive safely.

We stare out the car.
The snow is rain for a while
and then slush. I find where we are
on the map. Mother is silent while she drives.

And it is silence which falls
with more snow. I don't care, I must speculate.
Mother ignores my silence and calls
the weather awful when at last we pull over.

My dear girl! My sweet friend!
I compose to you in the hissing dark,
you are a poker player to the end,
your breasts are mushrooms without stems . . .

We try the engine again.
It coughs but it is frozen and out
of gas. I see the shapes of moving men
blanket the windows, they rattle the fender.

Mother! Ghosts! She finds an old
tartan traveling rug and lies down in
the back. Get some sleep, I am told.
Her breathing goes quiet and regular.

No ghosts. I can conjure up though
wide-eyed fevers to sweep the nation and
bloody betrayals and grotesque obesities and low
heaps of wrecked trucks and other violence.

What I picture comes true—their livestock frozen in the snow
and polar bears in our once-warm houses
and the creaking of glaciers and a wild ice floe
and death and flames in the desperate cold.

Only once during the night I tried the radio;
it was dead, and once I dreamed I was on the phone
to my sweetheart. Believe me, I said, I can't just go,
with the frostbite I've got, and hush my mother's still sleeping.

Second-Hand Clothes

More than a familiar face, I knew him when young,
And now the world is his anteroom.
We're overrun by ancestors and associates, well-wishers from everywhere,
As we ponder the exact wording of these huge banners
Tacked out for our consideration . . . *yet meanwhile,* still unseen
You must watch the waxy telephone cradled between
Her anxious ear and suspicious mouth. And truly,
Her wary voice begins, truly typical scheduling begins here—
You and I are involved, though I contemplate marriage no longer.

I have fought for this, on billowing office
Furniture, my trouser creases indistinguishable in the gloom
Of early winter, and pitilessly exposed by sharp fluorescent spring.
My letter of 12th August remains unanswered
And perhaps unopened on your desk, yet still
The billboards flicker, and I feel a rough hand
Flex, and prepare, somewhere in the vicinity of my shoulder.

Unpicking the Knot

Pot plants unwatered on the sun deck
Like moaning minnies lie down and die.

Her lips have twisted into a random smile, but
In her mind she curses in her mother tongue.

The room is now an inverted fish tank;
Things float helplessly up toward the glass—

Her brushes, her combs, her trash,
Objects it were useless even to list.

Each noise fades away like forgotten
Sex, its stripes etched faintly on the buzzing air.

You dream of a crisp welcome, leading into some
Precise business proposals. A three-course

Luncheon will follow shortly after.

A Head for Heights

Therefore a host of madmen
Has grown to love this sunny spot
And the expansive view of the city it affords.
While I clatter shut the lid of our faded
Lunch box, you shelter your eyes from the dazzling horizon
That surrounds us, sprinkled with trees
And speeding toward us and the magnificent city
Spread out for us, like a map, on the brown
Bumpy plain at our feet.

But where do they come from
These early voyagers of spring, hushed
And stricken and camouflaged among the waving trees?
No one knows. And the gathering roar of exploding leaves
One hears behind them, in contrast, the sap
And hidden movements, brand us
Conclusively, I think; the rustling forest
Must provide fruit, and quiet pools for bathing.
But leaving aside this, how awkwardly you move,
My dear, forgetting my companion must be spryer
Than any monkey, with limbs immaculate, and a walker
Of great distances, and that day and night
You must continually seek to astonish me
With your vital gift for life.

The Queer Smell of Gas

The gray of 3 AM envelops her room again. Hush!
From its mountainous source the Thames
Inches its way toward Southend
Under a glaring, three-quarters moon.

To grasp more fully his insignificance
Man propounds new and ever stranger theories
Of language and evolution. Others object merely
That the sexual revolution has been betrayed.

The day after the deal, the TV off, I took up
My woods, remembering Finsbury Circus.
The will was not to be contested. In theory
All the chairs in this house are now solely mine to dispose of.

Policing Beaconsfield

He talks with his feet;
"Er—," he pauses before replying.

Two pale fish flap
Through the aquarium.

How often did he take
Mind-expanding drugs?

A twist of cirrus, drifting slowly
Across the white ridge.

She lies there unmoving;
Her straw, they think, needs changing.

We voters long to be abused.
We love the truly merciless decisions.

Soft Sift

A chill March wind blows through
The vogue for cultural references;
In a twist the sporting chance we momentarily
Enjoyed is shut up like a geometry box.

Even the trees groan at the thought of standing
The test of time. Already a new challenger
Spars for an opening, the coordinates slide around
Like the proverbial vole in an hourglass.

And now beneath my cummerbund I feel
The familiar drain through the glands to the various pits.
I have etched kohl above my eyelashes.
Somewhere there is a problem, a rain-streaked mangle

Waiting in some yard for its unlikely delivery.

Coastal

From afar I saw where we were
And how his predilections had changed
On the hills, the gray sea, and the rocks.
And from this you see, how, when I move
Through the thinning air, I take note, and follow
Like a pup, obedient on the sand . . .
                                        Now
The lovely clapboard fades, the abandoned coves
And fishing smacks, and I can feel the dirtiness
Like gold thick on my palm, the rubbish
I shift into the piles at which I stare.

Affirmative Action

In the original raree-show, of which this is a pale
Imitation, phantoms swore and hurled mountains at each other;

Tiny, endless columns of red-jacketed soldiers
Adjusted their busbys before attacking a farmhouse;

And "White Light/White Heat" blared
From bank upon bank of shuddering loudspeakers.

Now a vast customer complaints department
Imposes everywhere its blinkered theories of art.

Come on, Government! You're supposed to be in charge!
What about these here hooligans running naked through the streets?

What about the stream winding through pleasant meadows
And the cows brooding in the grass?

What about midges, and toffee-apple, and washing days?

A Close Friend

She thought it might be vitamins.
I thought, rather, here was a man
Determined to waste his life.
We met in a bar to discuss tactics.
"He's alright," she declared in a whisper,
"Quite brilliant often." I asked her what she thought
Of his prospects. "Qu-qu-qu-quite good,"
She said. "Oh no!" I said,
"Don't tell me you've picked up his stutter!"

In the Adirondacks

Bumbling with a jackass haircut through the stormy weather
With my two companions, both fresh and witty—after a while
We were introduced, formally, and after that I enticed them on
With promises of extra time. Our two bloods fought,
The bloods of moraine and of ether, admiring the prospect
Exactly where the heavy snow covered the peaks and valleys, and lay
    waiting
For my perspiring friends to relax, and call for a new enterprise, a halt,
    an explanation,
Or indeed for me to kick their stubborn behinds . . .
I thought—like a thorn—here is my weary foot thudding through
Their winter padding, its neat quilts and roughened oilskins,
Fierce with exhaustion and contempt! I ripped
The gaudy strings of pearls from around their necks.
I derived no solace from stripping their mounted layers of clothing
Nor from exposing their healthy bodies to the wind.
Now, as I write, with my own pen, wifeless, rich, and comfortable,
With how little pleasure do I recall that disastrous vacation in the
    Adirondacks.

High Performance

Seaweed drips from one's head
Looking like hair—only green, straggling,
And with innumerable pods to pop.

Together we wander on through this literary-critical
Conundrum. We've spoken of it before
And have agreed we'd die for less.

It's all in the name of "high performance,"
Which really means good looks, a super intelligence,
And one of those tight-fitting, wavy-patterned sweaters.

A Swimming Pool Full of Peanuts

A stifling blanket day out west I was working the desert states
nothing for days thank you ma'm door slams in my face (again)
so I mosey out round the back where my vehicle sits melting I'll
just check the setup the outhouses the grass is all stiff
and plastic the trees are all lifeless and there's no shade
nothing stirring until I come across right in the open
a whole swimming pool full of peanuts I think
I've gone mad so I shut my eyes and I count
to five and look again and they're still resting there
very quietly an inch or so I suppose below
the high-water mark they're a light tan color
and the tiles around are a lovely cool aqua-blue
only there's no water just these peanuts.
Well this is a hoax I can tell some monkey's idea
of a good joke for who'd fill up a fair-sized swimming
pool entirely with peanuts unless they're painted in
which case it's a nice piece of work so I
kneel down in my best suit on the edge
(tie at half-mast because of the heat)
and with a loud snigger I dip in my finger
just to see it sinks into small grainy nuggets
sand-coated and a bit greasy some whole some in
half I draw it out and examine it all shiny with oil
the nail gleaming and I lick it to find out the taste
SALT! madness! the genuine article! straight salted peanuts!
this gets me because what kind of mad case goes
to the trouble of building a swimming pool and then fills it
instead of with water with salted peanuts right up to the brim

I'm the butt of his jest this goop is taking the Michael
almost physically I can feel him pulling my leg so
I lean over again and lower my head carefully until my
left eye is level with the glistening expanse for no
reason I'm feeling all queasy this pool full of peanuts
is disturbing my eye won't focus in case in an instant
they turn into piranha fish and green mambas
or anything else that might be hiding down there.

Still nothing moved I admit it was quiet too quiet
all I could hear was my own laboring breath
so in both clammy hands I scoop up fistful after fistful
and I watch them trickle through my fingers and glitter in
the sun I go back to my car and open up the trunk
I take out my golf bag I select a nine iron
and without a thought for my own safety I head back
to the pool and I swing away reckless in that peanut bunker
I scatter peanuts like a madman all over around there
they go flying like sandflies in all directions like golf
balls they arc away and shower down like buff-colored hail
and I thresh and flail like one possessed
but nothing is uncovered it's no good from the edge
so feet first I leap in at the deep end
brandishing my golf club and hit away
like a good soldier but there's more and more always
though I swing a good hour at the end of that
I am exhausted and my skin itches from the salt
and my clothes are all clinging I collapse in the middle
buoyed up by the peanuts the whole thing is hopeless
my pores are all clogged so I say let sleeping dogs lie

and I crawl to the side and haul myself out and
shake out the loose peanuts from the creases of my suit
I pick them out of my socks and empty out my shoes
I brush them out of my armpits and angrily I throw
my nine iron into the middle of the pool where it sinks
without trace and I storm back to my car and
I make this resolution never ever if you can ever avoid it
fool around with a swimming pool like this one
well a swimming pool full of peanuts is not worth the trouble.

Cross Section

We all knew of his exploits—
The flowers from the dean's wife for his overhead,
The chair carved into an oak tree bearing his name,
And the day he passed his driving test
Wine in hall for all.
                         A songster
Left out in the rain trills bleakly
It's morning: new habits for me too,
Sawing things palely in half on my sawhorse
Each Sunday afternoon.

Kid Crazy

Rangers patrol these woods. Orange discs
Mark their favorite trees, by which
They lie, between roots smothered in moss.

Each visitor takes home a scrap
Of bark. Their names
Are entered in the way station's register.

Supplies must be hauled in
By especially bred packhorse
Across a treacherously cratered terrain.

When a gaucho mops his brow with the hem
Of his singlet, all eyes seek out
The source of his implacable tattoos.

Super Black Thursday

Intense pressure builds up
In the sinus, making the legs
Weightless, the eyes water.
Beside me my mug, enameled,
With its slogan; its star signs
In tea leaves.
        The screen's blip
Has all but vanished. Green graphics
Reveal all—how here I wept,
There you scratched yourself,
On this estate I grew up, denting the garage doors
With my ball.
        PM. The newcomer's swivel chair
Lolls empty: across the city
Terminals are ablaze with the absurd news,
The markets shooting out in all directions,
In random, jagged leaps. Your eyes are
Seized by dysfunction. Then on this
Super day we gathered together, shouting,
Drank beer in flocks, somehow wheeled home
Reeling with it, breathing it all in, the night,
The ghostly carriage cloth, the stations blurred
And moving, always moving.

Demise

Rodents swarm over the earth; even Natty
Bumppo is taken aback. Scrambling eggs
Or brewing up porridge, he angles
The pan crazily over the fire.

Why bother to know about anything
Except the signs of the forest? Hark!
A Mingo moves stealthily on his custom-built
Moccasins from bush to bush.

Are we all thus accursed? The muzzle
Of La Longue Carabine pokes
Through the foliage; the sun gleams
On the frontiersman's mouse-colored rifle.

Then She Said She Had to Go

The drawing room was full.   The commuters half-turned
At last the angry hostess   to wave good-bye to
approached and   their friends. About their
whispered   feet fell the
black words
into my   of their
unsuspecting ear.   evening newspapers.

My new cow   Lunch is a strange experience
is loose in the field   here. The big hall is
With her tail she   full of birds
swishes   swooping around—
away flies
and wanders   a carrot I
happily to the fence.   was about to eat.

A large sea swell   The desk was littered
swamped the bay;   with books. She banged
the streets were   the front door, and I tried
drenched, and   to imagine
salt water
was found as   flowing
far inland as Newton.   from her lovely eyes.

Funny Peculiar

I sit down here drinking hemlock
While terrible things go on upstairs.

Sweat creeps like moss outward to the palms,
And time itself seems a strange, gauze-like medium.

Sleep will leave still newer scars each night, or,
Infuriatingly, is a curtain that refuses to close.

On the horizon, bizarre consolations make themselves
Known—a full fridge, a silent telephone,

The television quiet in its corner.
Everything and nothing have become a circular

Geometrical figure, seamlessly joined,
To be wrestled innocently this way and that

Into the most peculiar almost whimsical shapes.

Last to Leave

Things not necessarily funny
will stick in the memory, like recipes
for success, or how one once stood up
laughing, happy, a chip off the old block;
and I too, some days, rise, the applause
of the dying committee still ringing in my ears,
addressing absent friends, and those present,
for better or for worse, the tears now pouring
openly down my ravaged face. It's as if
our spirits merge, and the collection plates are
overflowing into the last few minutes
of the time remaining, as unknown guests
prowl through the empty bedrooms searching
for the stoles, fur hats, and winter coats
they deposited somewhere earlier in the evening.

Manifest Destiny

Apologies are for the birds.
The only way out is down
Through the earth—hence the slight
Squint and the furred paws like a mole's.

You meanwhile are immersed
In your bubble bath. Minor aches and pains
Dissolve in the soothing aromatic foam. Steam
Mists over the bathroom's several mirrors.

Like a trapper the spirit of freedom
Stalks the land. Already the generous
Pioneers respond with small cries, and
Tears, and heated haggling over suitcases.

Chattering Teeth

My teeth may chatter
But how I love her.
On frosty nights her silhouette
Dances against the brown barn door
Mocking me for something I might have said to her
During the day.
I follow the glittering points of the moon
Caught in her eyes,
Weaving toward me where I lie in the hay
Amazed at her dark moving arms
When all else is quiet asleep,
Only she in the silence
Flinging her legs in random cartwheels,
I hear clearly the touch of her bare feet
In the straw, lightly pressing the wooden boards . . .

But by dawn the stars are fading, and the mule
Is restless, wanting attention.
Such weather we're having, it won't last,
I remark out loud to myself, shivering, and watching
The sky, and imagining snow
Descending from it like a blanket,
Drift upon drift, piling up
Like a dome, around the various doors,
The roof, the attic window . . .

Under the Bridge

A secret fund of rage
Frees him from all worldly obligations.
He casts it out like the nearby
Fishermen, propped on their wooden stools.

The girders rumble, the house lights opposite
Come on. Two dogfish have expired
In my landing net. The madman
Has packed up his rod and tackle and gone.

Resting Up

Every high-rise has a special feel to it.
My window opens out onto some of the few
Miserable mean tearaways still left to sweat
The length of this big dipper,
But for me, no. In summer
I like to lie unbuttoned on my bed, and to
The tune of distant traffic I begin to scan
Page after page of any book I chance upon
In search of the shape of certain favorite words.
Nothing happens when I find them,
Maybe my lucky stars loosen up a little,
But it's hard to tell their shifted constellations
From the gentle flap of curtains in the cooling breeze.
I'll check for footprints in the sweet powdery dust
Banked along the window sill, and sprinkle birdlime on the ledge outside,
Then evening falls—maybe I'll wake up one day
Covered in white fluff, and with a fat pigeon nesting on my feet!
"Lie back and think of anything"
I tell myself on these occasions, to relax my mind;
I need so much food, so much sleep, just so much sun
And exercise, to firm me up and improve my touch.

Ledgers

Accordingly, I lay with my wife for three
Successive nights. During this exact period of time
The Mets beat the Cubs and it rained continuously.

October 8th. Fearful itching all over.
After much prodding and goading from H.
I agree to see a skin specialist.

The park by starlight. The margins
Fill with doodles. This space, these
Pages, shelve ever more steeply into darkness . . .

Outing

Ever since a willing spirit took me up
and began work on my reflexes, it feels
like I'm living the life my ancestors lived, though
I always imagine them as a wealthy jungle-dwelling people,
forever under the dripping elms.
If only it were truly impossible, and less like being a huge green amphibian
made to inch my homesick coils between the different counters
of your favorite store, taking all these fancy cautions
to keep my head down, and out of other shoppers' way.
Your ankles I can just make out. The cash till rings,
though I'll never know what you at last decided on
out of so vast a choice of things, quite naturally
you refused to wait until the crush thinned out.
The dusty floor is cool, like a fountain,
worn smooth and comfortable by so many feet.
The trusty bellboy follows obediently in your wake . . .
Now as I glide toward the whirr of sliding doors, I half hope
its electric eye won't respond to my irregular approach. Another
spanking clean threshold! "Open Sesame," it cries, "Hold tight!"
in its familiar southern drawl. "You know me well,
I won't be going to go to Hell for anybody."

FROM

SOFT SIFT

2001

.

Looping the Loop

Anything can be forgotten, become regular
As newspapers hurled in a spinning arc to land
With a thump on the porch where Grandma sits
And knits, her hound dog yawning at her feet.

And other strangled details will emerge and prove
Suddenly potent to confound the wary-footed, and even
The assembled members of the panel; in turn
Each pundit speaks, yanks from the hat an angry rabbit who flops

In spurts around the circular paths of crazy paving.
No pressing need to watch them but you do.

* * * * *

Dirty fingernails in August, and just
The amount of lightning threatened; superb
Courtiers sweep through the various precincts
Fingering each other's beads in the jagged dusk.

I myself went and left like a moron, but heard
The rumors nevertheless—meanwhile the wind
Pounds this shack with wilful abandon, then inquires,
As it eases, just exactly how many spliffs there were

Stashed that night in the cicada-colored
Pencil case tucked in the side pocket of her satchel.

* * * * *

Harsh truths indeed! I act the part of my own
Nemesis, polite, dazed, addicted to adversity,
Frequently drunk. Overhead the wires hum
Obscure ultimatums, mutterings that threaten

To aggravate forever these ordinary feelings, and inflict
Upon the world quantities of crazily worded postcards
Sent off on impulse from decaying seaside towns. For I still
Love the tang of brine, the old women hurtling on motorbikes

Through swirling banks of fog, any who loiter
Resentfully about the war memorial on summer afternoons.

*   *   *   *   *

Eventually one hears the cuckoo's call, while friends
Recline in armchairs. Let's off then, backwards through
The fisheye lens, bone by bone, clean shirts
Soon streaked and torn. Some fought like lovers

Under the bluish lights that swayed so weirdly
On their stanchions of pale, unpainted metal: how
Suddenly the team began to perform as if a stranger
Watched and cared, blindly probing through the endless rain

For openings, reeling back aghast, bitterly dispersed
One dank October, the sediment settling as best it might.

*   *   *   *   *

Afloat on the flood, indifferent to the cries
And the silence, I imprison your wandering hand:
In it lurk anecdote and polemic entwined, scars
Faint as a plate's, the luck of the stars . . .

Yet the affect hardly emerges, peers forth
Like a strayed mole through a cliff crevice
On the unfamiliar scene; though I have leapt and held
And carried, grimaced sourly at the brimming heavens,

A few feints and the incident spirals
Beyond reach, turns turtle in dreams displaced before morning.

Plan Nine

The dreadful telephone again: gentle as a kitchen
He'd walk through snow to lay his wreath or convey
Misgivings. The signal fades, freeing me to crawl
Through cold Friday, to forage amid the shadows cast
By a reckless crowd of brittle soap-opera characters.
Our bodies drag, halt mesmerized, lurch forward
With a yelp. "What's the story, morning glory?"
Inquires the super, whose reign of terror
And mind like glue leave less than ever
To be desired. I drink my Rhenish, though it tastes
Of poison, and attack with everything
Until at last the bugle sounds. Briskly, beyond
These streaming drapes, a caustic voice unfolds the case
To a clutch of bright-eyed interns: no mohair, no alcohol,
Lots of plain yogurt certainly, no foreign languages, no tête-à-têtes.

The Great Divide

The teapot slips from the hand. Some
Muscular ache lies patterned on the floor in irregular
Fragments of china; beyond, through the narrow meshes
Of twilight, children's shriekings filter and drain.

Raw fingers' ends search the delicate scalp.
Can these be stray traces of argument
Lost forever to posterity, while delays
And distractions alternate like checkered shade?

In an ill-fitting suit, heart pounding, one
Frowns at the herald's summons. Nothing moves,
Though a fleck still troubles the eye that absorbs
The scene, the shards, the gaudy colors of formica.

Contingency Plans

On balance it wasn't so much the cash
I was owed, as the attacks on my character; I
Prayed for deliverance and revenge. November
Lingered on gloomily: colds and fevers swept
The population, reduced swathes to troubled brooding
And red, streaming eyes; in a quandary I seized
My innate Englishness, and practiced
Wrapping it around me like an old army coat.

Two strikes, it was decreed, and you were out: appeals
For clemency were received with merry scorn.
As the gridlock eased I changed the subject,
Knowing my father, knowing the trees and the turnings and the signs
Along the route, and remembering his aversion to all
Blockages; I felt the engine growl, then
Shudder and forget itself. "I'm a Rhinestone
Cowboy" rode bucking and spangled across the airwaves
That spread like contours above the country's bumps
And hollows. A buzzing, roving helicopter eyed
The progress of our orderly parade; it would swoop
When necessary, a featherless scavenger lured by carrion.

The Long Man

of Wilmington winces with the dawn; he has just
endured yet another mythical, pointless, starry
vigil. His ankles ache, and the weather looks
irksome and moody: the early traffic whizzes by
regardless, but the news and emblems borne
by each car permeate the soil that sustains
the straggling furze, various grasses, and the odd
towering oak. Across the damp fields a distant
siren pleads for attention; he cannot
move, nor, like a martyr, disprove the lie of the land.

Who was it who established, in the teeth
of so much evidence, the laws of diminishing
returns? I woke up feeling cold and distended,
my feet pointing east, my head in low-hanging
clouds. A stream of curious tags and sayings
flowed like a potion through my veins. I had
the "look," as some called it, meaning I floated
in an envelope of air that ducked and sheered
between invisible obstacles. The alarmed
senses struggled to respond, then bewailed
the absence of detailed, all-powerful
precedents: I kept picturing someone tracing
a figure on the turf, and wearing this outline
into a path by walking and walking around
the hollow head, immobile limbs, and cavernous torso.

Jack Rabbit

Will I ever catch up, or will I be easily
Caught first? It was assumed I'd branch out
With the heretics, commit a few crimes, then
Suffer the decreed punishment; instead, I paused
Near the knoll where the vociferous and well-
Groomed gather to consider their options. I yearned
To wade through buttercups and clover toward
The sinister squadrons of an embattled
Bourgeoisie. Vivid mottoes—*One Size Fits*
Nearly All!, No Grammar, No Furniture!, Le Temps
Viendra!—still adorn the half-built walls. Prodigal
Sons and daughters stream forth in search
Of business, clutching their coats, bewildered by doubts
And strange aches; a thin layer of soot powders the buildings
They pass, and the cracked bark of the peeling plane trees.

*   *   *   *   *

So I reckoned to get quicker, leaner, braver, more
Self-effacing; I'd pick my way between
The mounds of junk cast off by warring factions, cleverly
Disguised and idly humming. I swam midstream
With the freshwater boys, and lounged on rocks
At evening. Meanwhile the air slowly thickened
With intrigue. Blueprints and memoranda
Began to circulate like the seasons, melting
The obdurate, blossoming where least expected:
We were to police ourselves, produce

Solemn recommendations, fall on our own
Swords. Wishes were transfigured into parables
And omens. Neither threats nor Chinese burns
Demolished my cloudy strategies, though a tow-haired
Bullyboy still slouches at the edge of sight, killing time.

Early to Bed, Early to Rise

It was in Berlin you mixed up John and J. J. Cale,
And we found ourselves watching Jacques Tourneur's *Out of the Past* yet
   again.

I, on the other hand, confused Teniers the elder and Teniers the younger
In Amsterdam, where I saw Terry Gilliam's *Twelve Monkeys* on my own.

On the outskirts of Moscow we failed to distinguish clearly between
   Charles and Burl Ives;
Our punishment was to sit through Sergei Eisenstein's *Ivan the Terrible*,
   Parts I and II, twice.

I met a man in New York who couldn't tell the difference between George
And Zbigniew Herbert; his favorite film was Kenji Mizoguchi's *Ugetsu
   Monogatari,* which he insisted we see together.

In Cardiff I confounded Edward, Dylan, and R. S. Thomas;
To get over my embarrassment I went to a performance of Jean-Luc
   Godard's *Alphaville.*

People continually mistake the work of Antoine Le Nain for that of his
   brother Louis, even in Los Angeles,
Where most films are made, including Doug Liman's *Swingers,* which I
   recently saw for the first time, and really enjoyed.

Misguided Angel

Where will you ride in this minute that stretches
Its wings, and soars aloft, and turns into
An unplanned, devilish interval? Serial
Misadventures have shattered the grip
Of barbed rubric and corporate logo; enigmas
Swarm at the brink of the five senses. When revealed
Each unlikely event exacts the stipulated
Blood money, bequeaths boils and frets and fresh
Starts. Whirled from place to place and buffeted
By crosswinds, the sorrowing imp struggles on, gloomy
As the impending thunderheads: Reflect, he insists,
On these peculiar facts; there is no controlling
One's renegade thoughts, nor striking
The fetters from blistered limbs. Inflexible etiquette
Demands every gesture be also a memory: you stare
Into space where fractions and figures still pursue
Their revenge; half-veiled by fumes, a lurid
Sickle moon unsettles the foundering traffic. Whoever claims
A stake out there must rise and speak in guttural tones
Of all they mean—or meant—to do, and why, and where.

Hooked

then thrown back, like a long-finned, too bony
fish, I finally took
him at his word, and felt the lateness
of the hour acquire a dense, rippling
aura that weighed down these eyelids, pressed

apart membrane and nerve: howsoever I twist
and retreat, I thought, or silently glide from
sphere to sphere, the merest
splinter of rage keeps returning as a glittering, razor-
edged weapon, and even after dawn

has tightened still further the angle between
reflex and use, a sort of sunken
tide pushes open my ducts, washes through
or else over uncertain
crumbling defenses, dissolves into itself whatever

floats, like quicklime, filters the air through fluids thicker, heavier
than water . . . as in a riddle, my entire
active vocabulary scatters and drifts, sucked
under, worn smooth to the touch; instead, circling
cries and swirling, opaque

graffiti scrawled in black
clouds of enormous letters come to seem
to define only their own unforgiving
and yet volatile laws: "Thou
yet behold'st me?" I'm half-inclined to bellow in jest

at the elements, but decide, inversely, my first
real maneuver must
be to conceal from the inquisitive, lopsided sun
the direction in which these currents are secretly
driving me, and the immaculate, tiny

moons that now cover my body.

I Wish

you would please spare me your Western logocentrism!
Isn't it clear I'm the sort who rejoices when the Queen Mother
chokes on a fishbone? I'd shine a harsh,
piercing light on the damage indiscriminately wrought
by the tinkling music of the spheres. Our errands merely *seem*
average and natural: every second is underwritten
by an invisible host of dubious connections; like phantoms
they flit and soar, then render unto Caesar what is Caesar's.

Others—I am not the first—have found themselves standing
on a seemingly solid patch of cliff that suddenly
starts to slide: as the knees tense and the hips swivel, the winding
path is transformed into a slalom. Through a blizzard of loam
and pebbles, oaths and jests, I tumbled toward the proverbially
treacherous soft landing. A flock of seagulls squawked
and fled, and I remembered a man who claimed he could speak
their language fluently: "Screeek!" he'd wail, "Screeek, screeek!"

As any newsagent will explain, it is only, alas,
when their businesses collapse en masse that they
themselves are the news. The public-spirited tear
open the serrated pages in search of names
long wreathed in puzzling, clinging mists, now ablaze
with fame. The print smudges the fingers. Streams
of disjointed syllables cleave the air, and threaten
the passerby who passes by, wrathfully, without flinching.

Reproduction

of whatever you are absorbing with your
five senses is forbidden, and may provoke
nausea, insomnia, loss of balance, or blurred
vision: it were better you retire, and then
attack, hurling weapons and imprecations
at the diffident foe. The world averts
its gaze, and unfortunate schemers drag
their woes from home to muddy fields: all
roads lead to rooms, as the Irish say, and
to windows through which one stares at the seething clouds.

One Indian summer, when the future
seemed to beckon with a double-jointed
finger, I took to loitering with uncertain
intent in the neutral, unblinking eye
of a slyly angled closed-circuit security
camera: when I yawned or stooped, somewhere
my grainy image followed suit. Shoppers paused
and threw me quizzical, sidelong glances. I perched
defiantly on the rim of a huge stone tub
of ferns, which I remembered, as they brushed my hair,
were thought by some to be about the oldest plants
on the planet. A portly, middle-aged
man in uniform, sporting mirror shades, ambled
toward me: I could tell he was bothered by the unseasonable
weather by the way my own features stretched and loomed.

He Aims

his catapult, and broods. Quivering washing
festoons the neighboring gardens, and the sky lours
like a rival consortium, poised to swoop. "Be

afraid" is his weird sort of motto. At dusk
clear divisions unfurl and dissolve; deluded
insects plunge frantically into pools and wedges

of soft, dizzying light. Scaly, half-formed scabs
begin to itch, then burn. The argument flies either
over the hedge, or from A to B and back again.

        *   *   *   *   *

As a child's tongue probes a wobbly milk tooth,
one is drawn to the far-flung, imperishable scenes featured
in a company calendar: veldt, ice floes, desert, miles

of prairie. Under the gentle aegis of a wide-
angled lens, earth and sky exchange elaborate
favors. The grayish remains of an unlucky midge

streak the aureate canyons of Death Valley. A herd
of startled antelope gallops into the sunset: out
of frame a lion pursues, because his name is lion.

        *   *   *   *   *

The conflict never ends, though the crowd chants
for a while before filtering home. The seasons revolve,
bringing honor and disgrace: flickering strings of price-

sensitive data orbit the world like molten, almost
invisible meteors. Look up and tremble; while the tongue
slurs and mangles yet more, ever-vaguer

resolutions, the body is taking its ten, horribly
deliberate paces. Eventually, if only to break
the eerie silence, he turns, closes both eyes, and fires.

Twenty-Twenty Vision

Unwinding in a cavernous bodega he suddenly
Burst out: Barman, these tumblers empty themselves
And yet I persist; I am wedged in the giant eye
Of an invisible needle. Walking through doors
Or into them, listening to anecdotes or myself spinning
A yarn, I realize my doom is never to forget
My lost bearings. In medias res we begin
And end: I was born, and then my body unfurled
As if to illustrate a few tiny but effective words—
But—oh my oh my—avaunt. I peered
Forth, stupefied, from the bushes as the sun set
Behind distant hills. A pair of hungry owls
Saluted the arrival of webby darkness; the dew
Descended upon the creeping ferns. At first
My sticky blood refused to flow, gathering instead
In wax-like drops and pools: mixed with water and a dram
Of colorless alcohol it thinned and reluctantly
Ebbed away. I lay emptied as a fallen
Leaf until startled awake by a blinding flash
Of dry lightning, and the onset of this terrible thirst.

She Spears

a tender asparagus shoot, nibbles at intervals, then embarks
on an equivocal theory of what happened and why: It was as if
I were—to borrow the title of a lurid thriller—déjà
dead! I sank through layers of debris and deceit, gnawed
by regrets, in search of a viable interiority. All around,
weeds sprouted in plant pots: threads of cuckoo spittle
dangled from thick-veined leaves that had outgrown
their strength. As I fell, the severed nerve in my right
ring finger began to tingle, then ache; *my eyes,* as I remembered
writing, almost dazed by my own cleverness, in my first
story at school, *slowly grew accustomed to the gloom . . .*

What one sees—more or less—one finally gets, provided
it nearly fits, and is affordable: my funny body
still behaves like a brand plucked from a huge, fiercely
burning brazier. Just out of range, jocular opinion-
makers fiddle knowingly with their nostrils, and seem to think
they are immortal; a few, ill-fated maneuvers
later, I return to my booth, feeling neutral, neither sadder
nor wiser, but anxious about my jabs—tetanus, influenza
etcetera—and the laws of the jungle. According
to Flaubert, it is the various mélancolies du voyage, its piercing
disappointments that most exhilarate the true traveler.

Be that as it may, I found myself drifting from inner
suburb to inner suburb, without a car or pets, aside
that is, from sluggish clothes moths and faithful silverfish:
jug-eared La Vieille, my least favorite landlady, took

to calling me in jest the Empress of the Reef. During this time even casual jibes, or tiny acts of spite, used to make me weep. One rainy morning, the mirror brutally informed me that a) anything went, and b) one wrong move and I'd have no moves left at all. The moment, I knew, had come to wreak revenge on the glass, to watch my pupils diminish to dark floating stars, to leave only the room in the reflection.

Penumbra

Beneath an angular web of scratchings-out
Vagrant motives glow like phosphorus: low, creeping
Tactics deny or dissolve whatever lies
In their path. I lean into the wind that blows
Off the lake, and scours the sodden fields; the sky's
Reflections ripple between ruts and bumps. I plunge
Toward remote vanishing points, where one man's
Loss unravels and becomes another man's
Devastation. Streams of ravaged spores dip
And swirl, and disappear, while downy
Nettles shiver beside a bristling hedge. Crops,
Sludge, restless drifts of leaves absorb
The haggard light. Things ready themselves for a reckless
Leap of faith: as storm clouds hurry above the shadowy
Tree line, the contours between grow vexed and dim.

We Crave

attention, then come over all coy, and start fiddling
with watchstrap and buttons, or talking about a friend
of a friend who claims to own the world's largest collection
of aquarium ornaments, yet has no aquarium. In the mean-
time the tough-minded argue each of us is loved not
so much for his or her oddities, as in spite of them, or even
faute de mieux! Families form, squabble on long
car journeys, invent nicknames for strangers; the tires hum
their own tune, and in shimmering forecourts
the baked atmosphere presses from all sides, searing
the lungs. We commend, internally, the wisdom of the soft-
voiced tycoon who acquired the land, only
to flatten it, then skilfully divide it into distinct
yet related lots; a spongy layer of wood chips lines
the crisscrossing paths, and whispers faintly underfoot.

As it was drummed into me, I would drum it
into others: the art or science of management never
pauses, though it occasionally lies low, or enacts
retreat like a Parthian archer. Invariably, speed and stealth
take advantage of the famous, nonexistent "margin" poor
Herbert Pocket kept urging upon Pip; a sound decisive
as the whirr and double click of a computer mouse
signals the arrival of the inner bailiffs, and an era
of thrift. Listen harder, and through the virtual prison bars
comes swarming the buzz of creditors and debtors over
lunch, each pledging allegiance to the other, to knowledge,
to the mysteries of living on thin air . . .

The Casket

(after Apuleius)

"But—now listen!—on no account open this casket, however
Curious you may feel, Psyche, after it has been filled with divine beauty."

So spoke the inspired, prophetic tower. Psyche made her way
To Taenarus, where she obtained a pair of coins for the ferryman, and
    the required
Barley cakes soaked in wine and honey. There she began her descent
To the underworld; as the tower had instructed, she ignored
The lame drover and his hobbling donkey, made Charon take his obol
From her tongue, stopped her ears to the cries of the dead
Swimmer, spurned the crafty weavers at work
On their infernal looms, then soothed three-headed Cerberus with one
Of her sweet, dripping cakes. Finally she arrived at the palace
Of Proserpine, where she would not relax on the cushions the Queen
Proferred, and declined all food but a hunk of coarse, black bread.
    Squatting
At Proserpine's feet, she explained her commission from Venus; at once
The casket was whisked away to be filled in secret, then returned,
Sealed. On her swift journey back she used her other barley cake
To silence the rabid jaws of Cerberus, and again made hell's ferryman
Accept his payment from her mouth. But on regaining the white
Light of day she so adored, Pysche, although eager
To fulfill the task Venus had set her, suddenly fell prey
To temptation. "I must be mad," she mused, "to carry, like this,
Beauty, and not take a little for myself, to please my divine lover."
Accordingly, she opened the box, but found inside not beauty,
But nothing, or rather an evil, insidious coma, a thick

Cloud of drowsiness that suffused and invaded her limbs until she
   collapsed
Where she stood on the path, and there she lay, slumped like a corpse, fast
   asleep.

You Must

endeavour to abstain from these—he paused, and smiled—
indulgences; the market expresses the collective will
of traders who have lived through ravening epidemics,
tempests, and droughts. What look to the newcomer
like loop-holes turn invariably, in time, into elegant
Venus's flytraps; some greenhorn is forever
decrying the delicate equilibrium that makes possible
the flow of goods and events. Confine your accounts
to terse columns of figures marching sternly
into the wilderness, away from grieving family and friends.

I slept under strips of frayed curtain, in a room
that lacked furniture and resembled a false-
bottomed suitcase; at length I relaxed, only
then to discover how many of my treasured, once-
chronic ailments had either blistered or burst. Without
benefit of clergy the familiar and the unknown
kept colliding, and issuing ultimatums, like a pair
of generals at war in a crumbling grammar: "Let battle
be joined; our envoys have returned empty-handed;
the enemy will sooner die than submit to the yoke."

What is more, within the year, each and every hopeful
ends up learning never to answer questions posed
in letters, and how to turn the other cheek, or sharply
on one's heel. In late spring, cockroaches stir
and swarm from house to house: costly, futile
efforts are made to curb their sallies. Debts and profits

accumulate, each driving the imagination to expand
into distant, untouched regions. One shivers
or sweats, as the seasons break and fronds and tendrils
turn into wallpaper, and wallpaper into tendrils and fronds.

Arrowheads

Spring rain seeps
    between leather
        upper and sole,
           darkens the scabs
              of rust lining
                the crevices
                of a green Hillman
I say "I," yet all I am is a specter haunting some weedy, abandoned estate.
              order on behalf of the
          a voice called for
       like seabirds until
     milled and cawed
   nephews and nieces
  cousins, distant
Brisk, ebullient

          it here: Horatio!
        but will practice
      I find this difficult
    by his first name;
  to address him
 begged me twice
R—has now
Mister was her nom de plume, or rather spray can, the police revealed.
 Mister he might
  have been called
   for he was an old-
    style outlaw,
      a saddle and trigger-
       happy hero, the last
        genuine hombre.

Snags and Syndromes

Our collective reverie, a lost soul ventured
To explain, is about as random as the ebb
And flow of the stock exchange: we're so easily
Suckered we no longer care. The head and ears
Throb incessantly, and our spoofs and ripostes
Either fall flat, or degenerate into pleas
For sympathy. It becomes clear that each flaw, from
The structural to the trivial, must end up taking
The shape of a triangle: our schemes sink
Into the marl like arrowheads, then rear
As Satan in a pyramid of fire. Under duress, our
Verbs stammer and yield to an unknown third person singular.

*   *   *   *   *

Ignoring all this, I sauntered forth, past a dog
Rattling his chain, autumn crocuses, vacant benches,
And tree trunks scarred with initials. A blue, dripping wet
Bag winked in the arms of a sycamore; squirrels
Worried among twigs and roots half-hidden
By twitching leaves. Someone, I noticed, had drawn
Boxes for hopscotch, then left the chalk itself
Lying in the penultimate square. Continuing, I stumbled
Upon the "main drag," to borrow a term
Of my mother's. Cars, shops, and pedestrians merged
Into one; I heard my name whispered fiercely, excitedly,
In a voice I both dreaded and instantly recognized.

Inside

There are wheels within wheels, he yelled
At the wall, and within those wheels
Are tiny images, untitled books, desperate
Or creepy entanglements. The arrowheaded cursor points

Into space, but glides like a shark between
Sandbar and reef. I think of the pods, the soft
Fissured matter that makes up the brain, and how
Lightning forks and tears through swollen

Layers of cloud, burns like a tattoo in a far corner
Of the retina; reeling, in a cross-eyed
Fleeting trance, I'd feel I peered through jagged, hairline
Cracks in air into streams of spiralling, contagious fire.

                    *   *   *   *   *

November 3rd. Cast aside all fears, all inhibitions
And *worked*. Also—but neutrally—happened to remember
Today is the anniversary of our long-forgotten neues
Leben: having dipped first a toe, then my entire

Being in pure solvent, I am either
Numb as wood, or myself pure spirit. Mid-
Morning I paused, and heard the sharp clippety-clop
Of a police horse's hooves suddenly drowned by a car

Alarm's wailing. Left alone, inclined never
To complain to doctor, landlady, salesperson

Or lawyer, it is only in theory that I've no
Time or money, am open like a street map to the enemy.

*   *   *   *   *

A new regime, supposedly, and even darting, bright-feathered
Rumor is lost for words, fidgets and flutters, each
Shifty eye pleading for shelter; in a prolonged fit
Of absentmindedness I end up conceding point

After point, unable to resolve how to stem or else
Ride the ruthless, intricate currents as they
Flood then recede, burying the nerves under layers
Of heavy silt, sand, pollen, and rotting leaves. Another

Squinting sun, another set of assumptions to watch quiver
And disband: while fragments of a searing, inadmissible
Question blister the tongue, earth and air appear
Fused in a permanent dusk, the hour entre chien et loup.

"Stop Knocking . . ."

(after Charles d'Orléans)

Stop knocking for entrance to my thoughts
Care and worry, spare your knuckles,
For my brain is sleeping, and not to be woken—
Last night, you see, was spent in pain.

I must relax or I'll succumb, brain-fevered,
Please, please allow this poor mind rest.
Stop knocking for entrance to my thoughts
Care and worry; spare your knuckles.

As a cure Bon Espoir has devised
And had prepared a certain medicine:
I cannot lift my head from this pillow
Until I've had, at last, enough sleep sleep sleep . . . now
Stop knocking for entrance to my thoughts.

FROM

SIX CHILDREN

2011

Dominion

Rise up! we heard their war cry—*Levitation!*
the trembling leaves kept sighing—
Levitation! Then Hurry Harry abandoned
the way of the raccoon and beaver, and felt
his heart whirled aloft by some hand
or talon: Oh no more, he reasoned, will I scramble
blindly between settlement and clearing, mocked
by the melancholy loon. Off—off—again
off, ye buckskin garments! How it glints,
my rifle, in the sun, as it arcs
toward the lake. And listen—on the stony beach
the ripples whisper, *Oh hurry*
Hurry Harry, oh Harry, hurry, hurry . . .

The Death of Petronius

(after Tacitus)

Turning to Caius Petronius, there are a few things about him that deserve
To be remembered: he liked to sleep all day, then devote his nights
To business—or pleasure. Most have to work hard
To become well-known, but it was idleness that propelled
Petronius to fame. He differed, though, from most debauchee or wastrel types,
For he was a cultured, exquisite master of the subtle arts
Of indulgence. His way of speaking, his way of doing things, seemed always casual,
Fresh, and cool. Appointed governor of Bithynia, and then later consul, he also
    showed he could be an astute
And vigorous administrator.
                        At length, resuming his life of vice—or apparent vice—
He found himself taken up by Nero, and admitted into the Emperor's coterie
Of intimates. They dubbed him "Arbiter of Taste," and for a time Nero's sense
Of what was elegant or charming was determined wholly by Petronius. But this
So irked another of Nero's favorites, and voluptuaries, Tigellinus, that he hatched
A plot designed to appeal to the Emperor's overriding passion—
His cruelty. The Arbiter was framed
By a bribed slave, his household imprisoned, and his defence
Dismissed.
           Learning his fate
While at Cumae, Petronius at once abandoned
Both hope and fear—yet he refused simply to fling away
His life, either. Instead, having opened the veins
In his wrists, he'd let them bleed for a while; then, when the fancy
Moved him, have them bound up, then opened again, all the while
Chatting with friends about this and that, steering the conversation away
From serious topics that might make him seem brave

Or stoical. He lay back, listening to them recite
Not dreary reflections on the immortality of the soul or the nature
Of wisdom, but light songs and nonsense verse. Some of his servants
Received gifts, others a good flogging. Having dined
As usual, he slipped quietly into sleep—or was it death?—
As if it were the most natural thing in the world.
                                                    While many
Doomed like Petronius compose deathbed testaments that shamelessly flatter
Whoever happens to be in power, his will contained a list
Of all the Emperor's most peculiar erotic tastes and extravagant
Sexual experiments, and the names of his partners
In crime, both men and women, willing and unwilling. He sent this
Under seal to Nero, then broke his signet ring: it, at least,
Would be innocent of the blood of others.

The Gaping Gulf

Cloud-capped, deserted, building and building site
Exchange whispers and winks. I glide half-
Asleep down the alley between them, as if
Adrift on some superannuated schooner. Nearby, on another
Kind of scaffold, John Stubbs gallantly raised his hat to the cheering crowd
With his left hand, and blessed the Queen, while her
Executioner held aloft his right.
                                        Then he fainted. I've the taste
Of azure and wind in my mouth, and flecks
Of soot and dust in my hair. I think
Of all those on the verge of fainting
Today—teachers and alcoholics, long-distance runners, Tokyo-bound
Commuters crushed rib to rib. Their lungs
Wheeze and labor, and would rest; they need
A cold compress, a caressing breeze, some
Respite from the rattling drone of dried peas
In the inner ear. Ruminating, renouncing
Word after spellbound word, the alphabet looms like twenty-six
Patient camels on the horizon, then breaks
In half between the letters *m* and *n,* burdened
By too much grit
And rubble, and sand . . . Look! A sand-
Colored lizard is disappearing through a hair-fine
Crack in the wall just above the wireless, as one gropes
For the dates of the reign of Henry
The Navigator, or Philip the Second
Of Spain. Dusk
Descends here like a thrown cloak, coarse, thick, almost suffocating,

Alive with inexplicable sounds. Was that
A distressed owl, or the harsh bark
Of a disease-bearing fox? What bothered who- or what-
Ever cried?—distant thunder vexing the dim
Hyades, or breadfruit upon breadfruit thudding
To earth?
      The gulf
Between a bleeding wrist and the breadfruit-crowned
Adventures of the current Order
Of the British Empire, is fast receding into the dark
Back of time. My father (born October 1934, died
The last day of May 2007) kept his medal in a safe
Cleverly hidden in the utility room.
The institutions that formed him, bade him don
A tin hat at Suez, shimmer like elegant, gauzy backdrops
Floating down from the flies. He wept
Rarely, ate powdered egg through gritted teeth
As a child, believed in the beneficent
Stride of progress. "Who
Would true valour see," we sang
At the crematorium, "Let him
Come hither."

Six Children

"Though unmarried I have had six children." —Walt Whitman

The first woman I ever got with child wore calico
In Carolina. She was hoeing beans; as a languorous breeze
I caressed her loins, until her hoe lay abandoned in the furrow.

The second was braving the tumultuous seas that encircle
This fish-shaped isle; by the time a sudden riptide tore
Her from my grasp, she had known the full power of Paumanok.

One matron I waylaid—or was it *she* who waylaid
Me?—on a tram that shook and rattled and
Rang from Battery Park to Washington Heights and back.

O Pocahontas! You died as Rebecca Rolfe, and are buried
In Gravesend. Your distant descendant, her swollen belly
Taut as a drum, avoids my eye, and that of other menfolk.

While my glorious diva hurls her enraptured soul to the gods,
I sit, dove-like, brooding in the stalls; what in me is vast,
Dark, and abysmal, her voice illumines and makes pregnant.

Some day, all together, we will stride the open road, wheeling
In an outsized pram my sixth, this broken, mustachioed
Soldier whose wounds I bind up nightly. His mother I forget.

International Bridge-Playing Woman

where must you wander? Macao, the Moluccas, a spa
near Minsk, as far as Montevideo? Do the hands
you lost haunt you? In aerodromes
and embassies the cards were shuffled, dealt,
assessed, while catchphrases whirred and chimed. Under a comic
pith helmet his supreme Loneliness, the ace
of trumps, divided the continents and time zones, braved
assegai and fever, emerged trembling from the interior
like pure prestige. The picture cards
leered roguishly as the Emperor's Band slid
into *"There's a long long trail a-winding, into
the land of my dreams"* . . . One
fled what one was, and the house where the towels had always
to be hung straight on the towel racks: Since you must tear,
the quivering poplars whispered, yourself
bodily from your roots, let your thoughts
aerate and take wing; step
around the griffins, across the gravel, through
the dense, familiar shade cast by church
and church tower. May you
engage and defeat fear, strike even as home swells, blurs, or collapses
into a trick of air. While we
rustle and flex in the breeze, you will be floating
above squalor and sprawl, as remote and elusive
as a cloud. In the small hours,
in the lull before monsoon or typhoon
or insurrection or revolution, as the chambers of the heart
dilate, breathe in the night and let it stain

your blood, and obscure the lines
between black and red, chance and fate, abroad
and England. Either you belong
with those who belong, or you believe the stories
the cards tell, whether pieced together in windy
Mandalay, or in a small hotel tout près de la place Pigalle.

John Hall

Like Lord Cerimon he was familiar with the blest infusions
                That dwell in vegetives, metals, and stones:

He cured, he records, Michael Drayton of a tertian
                Fever with a spoonful of syrup of violets, and his own

Hemorrhoids with a pigeon he cut open alive, then
                Applied to his feet, to which it drew down

The vapors, while leeches set to work on his fundament.
                His beloved Susanna, Shakespeare's eldest, found

Relief from corruption of the gums and stinking breath, wind,
                Melancholy, and cardiac passion in his potent ointment

Of roses, capon grease, sweet almonds, and mallow water. Accounts
                Of his triumphs were kept in condensed Latin;

None of the cases published in *Select Observations*
                On English Bodies mentions his father-in-law's afflictions

Or demise. He himself died fighting a sudden and virulent
                Outbreak of the plague: "Health is from the Lord." (Amen.)

Lower Case

Using the heel
Of either hand, how I'd like to knock-
Knock-knock-knock some raw, devil-may-care
Spirit into the echoing chambers
Of the brain. Around
My cranium the churned-
Up air falls still, is hushed, save
Where the weak-eyed bat, with short
Shrill shriek
Flits by on leathern wing, tiny against the violet
Evening sky, or a scything blur
Across the twisted boughs and the white, waxy flowers
Of the frangipani trees.
                              Meanwhile, a blast
Of Shelltox
Dispatches another cockroach—it flips
Over twice, and its legs
Stop moving; its shiny brown shell, now beaded with poison, looks
Like a chain-smoker's nail. Through
A drifting mist of insecticide I hover
And roam, index finger
On the trigger, until the bitter fumes fade, and my interest
In killing what Shelltox kills
Fades . . . Relax
O muscles, in arms, neck, eyes, and face—cast
Out remorse for this and other
Fits that wrench, wrench
And squeeze, squeeze and catch

In the throat. Let no man
Squirrel away what he owns, or thinks he owns, nor, ill
At ease in his own skin, swallow fire and so
Burn inwardly. As a fly
Eludes a motionless gecko's
Quicksilver tongue, and the whine of the generator
Dies away, I feel emptied, lighter
Somehow, as alert
As a blood-hungry mosquito; the heart's
Fibrillations are the earth
Turning, while my thoughts
Float free and under
The cool bristling grass, the damp stems
Disappearing into stringy roots, the tunneled soil and gritty sand
And clay.
   Relax
O muscles, squirrel
Nothing away; let the churned-up air fall still,
Though a trigger finger hovers
In the violet night, a quicksilver, scything
Blur.

The Death of Hart Crane

Sir/Madam,

I was intrigued by the letter from a reader in your last issue that recounted his meeting, in a bar in Greenwich Village in the midsixties, a woman who claimed to have been a passenger on the *Orizaba* on the voyage the boat made from Vera Cruz to New York in April of 1932, a voyage that the poet Hart Crane never completed. According to her, Crane was murdered and thrown overboard by sailors after a night of such rough sex that they became afraid (surely wrongly) that he might have them arrested when the boat docked in Manhattan. This reminded me of a night in the early seventies on which I too happened to be drinking in a bar in Greenwich Village. I got talking to an elderly man called Harold occupying an adjacent booth, and when the conversation touched on poetry he explained, somewhat shyly, that he had himself published two collections a long time ago, one called *White Buildings* in 1926, and the other, *The Bridge,* in 1930. I asked if he'd written much since. "Oh plenty," he replied, "and a lot of it much better than my early effusions." I expressed an interest in seeing this work, and he invited me back to his apartment on MacDougal Street. Here the evening turns somewhat hazy. I could hear the galloping strains of Ravel's *Boléro* turned up loud as Harold fumbled for his keys. Clearly some sort of party was in progress. At that moment the door was opened from within by another man in his seventies, who exclaimed happily, "*Hart!*—and friend! Come in!" The room was full of men in their seventies, all, or so it seemed, called either Hart or Harold. The apartment's walls were covered with Aztec artefacts, and its floors with Mexican carpets. It dawned on me then that Hart Crane had not only somehow survived his supposed death by water, but that his vision of an America of the likeminded was being fulfilled that very night, as it was perhaps every night, in this apartment on MacDougal Street. At the same instant I realized that it was I, an absurd doubting Thomas brought face-to-face with a miracle, who deserved to be devoured by sharks.

Yours faithfully,

Name and address withheld

The Passing of the Passenger Pigeon

This bird used to be the most numerous on Earth
And to blot out the sun for hours over Wisconsin and Michigan,
And to strip bare the great forests of cranberries, pine nuts, and acorns.

Whole trees toppled under the weight of roosting birds. In flight
They made a sound like Niagara Falls. Horses trembled,
And travelers made wild guesses at their numbers and meaning.

The bird's sad demise is chronicled on many websites. Children
Visit these for homework, and learn how far and fast the passenger pigeon
Flew, and that its breast was red, and head and rump slate blue.

As the opulent sun set, raccoon-hatted hunters would gather with pots
Of sulphur, and clubs and poles and ladders; in a trice they'd transform the dung-
Heaped forest floor into a two-foot carpet of smoldering pigeon.

Being so common, they sold in the city for only a few pence a dozen.
Farmers fed them to their pigs. By the century's end they had all
But joined the Great Auk and Labrador Duck in blissful oblivion.

The last known passenger pigeon was called Martha, after Martha
Washington. She died in Cincinnati Zoo on September 1st, 1914. Her stuffed
Remains were transported to the capital, and there displayed in the Smithsonian.

White Nights

(after Lucretius)

A snake, if a man's spittle
Falls upon it, will wriggle
And writhe in frenzied contortions, and may even gnaw
Itself to death; and there are certain
Trees, should you ever drift off to sleep
In their shade, you'd wake clutching your throbbing head as if an ax
Had been buried there. The blossom, I've heard, of a type of rowan
That flourishes in the mountains
Of Helicon has overpowered and killed with the vile stench
It emits. And women should be wary
Of the potent musk of the beaver, which can force a busy housewife
Suddenly to drop her darning, or her delicate needlework, and collapse
In a dead faint—though this
Occurs only if the scent is inhaled at the time when her menstrual
Blood is flowing.
                      Those afflicted with jaundice see everything
As yellow because their yellow bodies
Send out—like a halo or aura—a constant stream
Of tiny bright yellow seeds, and these seeds merge
With the images careering through the air from all that exists; and then a
              further
Coating of yellow is added by the patient's
Yellow eyeballs, which tinge all they absorb with their own
Lurid hue.
              We humans did not, in my opinion,
Long ago slide from heaven
To here on some golden chain; nor did we emerge

From the ocean, nor were we created by the relentless pounding of waves
On rocks. It was the earth
Which bred us, as she feeds us still. Out of her own
Sweet will she created the wheat that shimmers, laden
Fruit trees, and buttercup meadows. But now nature
Seems tired; our farmers exhaust their oxen
And themselves, they blunt ploughshare
After ploughshare, but to little avail. The soil yields what it yields
Grudgingly, and demands more and more labor.
The wizened farmer sighs, and can't help
Thinking back to the days of his father, when things
Were simpler, and the fields more fertile, though far less
Of the world was cultivated. Likewise, the vineyard owner
Broods morosely on his twisted, stunted
Vines, and curses heaven, not realizing
That all things decay, that all things sink
Toward the grave, grow frail or weary, are worn gradually
Away by the remorseless passing
Of the years.

The Snare Unbroken

A nobler subject asks th' advent'rous song, sang
Mather Byles, then bade the Muse on soaring
Pinions rise. Goliah had to be defeated. In a secret

Haunt far removed from all the restless, glaring scenes
Of day, he communed alone, or with James Ralph
Observed the twinkling stars prepare their circuits. How

He envied Cotton Mather, who'd heard the war whoop, and rejoiced
Over the rout of a band of roving Iroquois—*lo, their Mightiest*
Are quelled, Salvage and Sagamore lie overturned, and fiery

Foaming Blacks . . . their torsos, horridly streaked,
Their brawny flesh and prodigious bones, lay
Moldering in some dappled forest clearing, picked clean

Eventually by crows. O citizens, let's catch
And pluck one, or more than one, and with every ink-
Black feather write of infernal regions of despair,

Of ghastly smiles and lidless eyeballs; of glittering
Temples and gay cities built on arid plains
And swamps, of silver mantling the moon sublime, and of

The snare that Satan set, unbroken.

Signs of the Times

"Today," wrote Thomas Carlyle
As the brown and barge-laden Thames rolled past
Cheyne Walk, "I am full of dyspepsia, but also
Of hope." On the *Today*
Show today a dyspeptic interviewer set brusquely about
A hopeful minister, and I ingested, along with the dyspepsia
And the hope, a story about a dubious collector
Of Regency soft toys and Apache
Bows, arrowflints, and tomahawks. Next
In line to be scalped was a corrupt
TV game-show host. Whither
The gentle, humane
Quizmastership of Magnus Magnusson, or the calm and bespectacled
Bamber Gascoigne?
                         Sweet day, so cool, so calm,
So bright, on which I don a shirt that cries out
For cufflinks, and sports
Embroidered initials on the right-hand cuff; on
Which I opened a desk drawer and discovered
A dozen or so pairs of sun-, half-rim-, and reading-glasses
Beneath an essay in progress on the French
Revolution, and notes
Toward another on the Spanish Civil War. We
Were born in the forward-
Thinking sixties, and grew up in various capital cities in Africa
And Asia—wherever, that is, the British Overseas Airways Corporation
(BOAC, for short) saw fit. In Lagos
The gardener earned a trifling bonus for each

96

Black mamba he destroyed
With his machete; they lurked mainly in the cool
Of the garage, curled behind the whitewall
Tires of our sturdy Zephyr, deaf to the shouting and rifle fire
Of the barracks adjacent, and military sirens tearing
Open the heavy heat.
                    It took—or seemed
To take—no time at all for the venom to prove, point
By careful point, what it meant. I found
Myself sweating too, trying
To recall the serpentine journeys made by adventurers such as Mungo Park
And Richard Burton, and the weeping jungles
And empty deserts they traversed. Unsheathed, their bone-
Handled bush knives whispered
Like settling locusts or long-
Promised waterfalls. One sticky morning
John Hanning Speke awoke on a spur above Lake
Tanganyika with a ferocious headache,
Blind as an earthworm. The clear lake waters rippled
And sighed, then flared like a peacock's tail
Beneath the whitening sky.

They Drove

just terribly, but humorously sang
Jonathan Richman's "Stop This Car" after each sudden

swerve or rubbery squeal. Once they discussed
the pros and cons of having sex

with Bob Dylan—or a Bob Dylan look-alike—in a Buick
while listening to "From a Buick 6."

Black fumes billowed from the exhaust, and by a species
of dead reckoning they charted, in a road atlas, detours

and punctures, losses and gains—all
the time wondering whether (as Van Morrison once

sang) to "Hardnose
the Highway" were the same as to live.

Hourglass

Early August, and the chestnuts
Are wilting—their splay leaves
Tattered and blotched, their shadows, not understood, speaking
A forgotten tongue . . . tell, tell us where, their drugged sap
Must be sighing, tell us where our distress
Ends, where
Are the victories? Each pinched, each
Aching hour we grow sadder
And stranger: a rift
In the billowing cloud cover, this cage
Of rain, soft grayish
Swarms of nameless insects circling, alighting,
Settling, sustaining themselves,
A sandy, pockmarked
Wormcast, the deft sideways hop
And jab of a predatory
Speckled starling—are the shreds and fraying
Filaments
An irresolute wind
Is teasing
Apart, winnowing
And dispersing, strand
By strand by strand.

* * *

"See," I grieved, "his mind
That so filtered

And sifted nature it made transparent her weirdest secrets, now lies
A broken prisoner of night. His neck
Droops, as if bowed with chains, and he sees nothing
But the cold, gaping ground." At this, fixing me
With her gimlet eyes, the strange woman answered: "But surely you
Are one of those who once lapped at my breast, and were raised
To tough-minded
Maturity on what I fed you? I armed you as well, yet you threw away
My weapons, not realizing
They would have kept you safe. Now
Do you recognize me? . . . You don't speak. Is it shame
Or stupefaction that keeps you silent? How I wish
It were shame!" Then, when she saw
My tongue and lips had utterly frozen, she approached
And laid a soothing hand
On my torso: "We must wait," she murmured, "for this fit
To pass. He'll know me soon enough, and then
Himself. For the moment let me wipe
Away some of the worries obscuring, like thick storm clouds,
His troubled sight." So speaking, she folded her dress
Into a pleat, and reached out, and with it dried my streaming eyes.

* * *

Through
The valley ran a brook
In full spate. I descended, and passed a middle-aged woman kneeling
At its edge. She was washing potatoes. When I travel, I travel
Light, with just a few things in a knapsack, no sword
Hangs from my belt. And with my shaven head

I look like a priest, but I'm not, for I'm powdered
All over, from crown to foot, with the dust
Of the world . . . I reached home
Just as the leaves
Were turning, and my brothers and sisters
Gathered round, excitedly; but all I saw were wrinkles, dewlaps,
White eyebrows, and watery eyes. My older brother
Pressed into my hand a small purse, and said,
"Open it." Inside were a few strands of white hair
Preserved in a tiny glass case as relics
Of our mother. Nothing was the same, and it seemed
A miracle we were ourselves
Still alive. While I balanced
The frail, intertwined hairs in the palm
Of my hand, I kept imagining my tears
Dissolving them, their melting as an early autumn frost
Melts in morning rain.

After Africa

After Africa, Surbiton:
An unheated house, and flagstone pavements;
No colobus monkeys, no cheetahs scouring the plains.
Verrucas and weeping blisters ravaged our feet.

An unheated house, and flagstone pavements,
And snow falling through the halos of street lamps;
Verrucas and weeping blisters ravaged our feet;
But the shavings made by our carpenter, Chippy, were as soft as bougainvillea
      flowers

Or snow falling through the halos of street lamps.
Everyone was pale, pale or gray, as pale or gray
As the shavings made by our carpenter, Chippy, which were soft as bougainvillea
      flowers . . .
Red, African dust spilled from the wheels of our toy trucks and cars.

Everyone was pale, pale or gray, as pale or gray
As the faded carpet on which
Red, African dust spilled from the wheels of our toy trucks and cars.
Real traffic roared outside.

A faded carpet on which
Everything seemed after Africa; Surbiton's
Real traffic roared outside—
No colobus monkeys, no cheetahs scouring the plains.

Ravished

Is the night
Chilly and dark? The night is chilly
But not dark. An all-but-full
April moon
Slides above barely visible clouds, and is greeted
By a burst of hooting from an urban
Tawny owl. On empty
Brownfield sites they nest, and rear their young, and feed
On vermin. Has
Any
Probing, saucer-eyed astronomer, even a modern
Or French one, ever
Grown genuinely accustomed "aux profondeurs du grand
Vide céleste"? Someone halts, and broods
In the deserted doorway of a Chinese
Emporium, someone
Is struggling to rise swiftly
From his chair.

* * *

A pair of empty
Curly brackets might have been
His colophon, I thought, parting one night
At closing time
On Great Russell Street, outside our last port of call, the Museum
Tavern. Between his thick-
Soled hiking boots rested a battered duffel bag with a single yellow

Shin pad protruding. A group
Of youthful partygoers sashayed by—one wearing a traffic cone
On her head: "*like*
A complete unknooown," a voice from the pack
Intoned . . . I was picturing the shiny black
Cab he so imperiously
Hailed whisking him west, revving, cruising, braking, gliding
Across junctions, the driver
At length twisting around, awaiting payment, as I veered
And tacked through the eerily silent
Squares of Bloomsbury, toward Euston.

Gregory of Nazianzus

stretched out on the grass, and tried
to relax. A delightful breeze stirred his beard
but his ear canals ached, and his tongue
felt bloated. While there is blood
in these veins, he mused, and I can hear
the murmur of leaves, and sparrows sing, I will not despair.

He half-dozed, and in a waking dream relived the despair
that had seized him during a stormy voyage from Alexandria to Athens.
      Death had tried
and tested him then. He'd shouted a prayer, but all he could hear
were the howling winds and surging seas, and the sailors cursing: "Your white-
      bearded
God seems a trifle deaf," one taunted; the blood
drained from his face, but he refused to hold his tongue.

"And once in Athens," he reflected, startled awake by a falling pinecone, "how my
      tongue
loosened, and poured forth God's word; even Basil despaired
of rivaling my eloquence . . . Basil . . . in Athens we lived together like blood
brothers, sharing cramped lodgings, frugal meals, our innermost thoughts . . . I tried
so often, to write to you . . . I see you now, your hair oiled, your beard
neatly trimmed, leaning into me, as if my words were all you ever wished to hear . . .

"Who lured me to Constantinople? that city of angels—and dogs! The people flocked
      to hear
the Holy Spirit move my lips, but many were swayed by the lies of that silver-tongued
viper, Maximus the Cynic, his glossy beard

all drenched with spittle and crocodile tears, his clothes rent in despair
at the hellfires being stoked for my followers. Brazen calumnies . . . yet when I tried
to refute them, the crowd hooted and hissed me, and hurled stones, drawing blood."

As the rays of the sinking sun slanted through cypress and pine, Gregory's blood
cooled. He thought he could hear
his houseboy shouting his name, and he tried
to respond but couldn't, for his tongue
seemed glued to his palate. He felt the slow encroachment of despair.
Something was crawling through his beard.

Gloomily he resumed his train of thought: "My poor beard
was not only matted, but stained a deep crimson with my own blood
as I cried to the Lord, not in despair,
but joyfully, believing He would hear
and gather me up, and that cherubim and seraphim would soon, and with one tongue,
be exalting me . . . now I fear I was tried,

tried and found wanting . . ." Stroking his beard,
he observed the flickering tongue of a lizard, and waited for the blood
to return to his own. He could hear his houseboy's cries receding, and in his voice a
note of despair.

A Natural History

> . . . the river's

Ice closes; silvery carp, whiskered and scaly
As dragons, cluster
And thrash around the piers
Of the bridge. Frogs,
Eels, water rodents
Die. On the bank, preserved like impurities
In glass, a rutty tangle of wheel tracks, of paw-
And hoof-prints, of sandal- and boot-prints. At intervals
I found fire-
Ravaged altars, some blackened, some
Still smoldering; pools
Of congealed blood, from either an offering or perhaps
A wound, lay in the hollows
Of the uneven floors. Near one
I knelt and fingered
The shards of a pot, or water clock, painted bright red
And pink, like a fuchsia; tucked
Up under the eaves of another, an abandoned
Bird's nest, fabricated in a curious manner
From scraps of wool, and brown animal hair, and a few fragments,
     torn but still
Just legible, of papyrus . . .

> . . . now the Magi

Who are all
Appalling liars, believe the gods will never appear to, nor obey,
A person with freckles. To one who has a fishbone

107

Lodged in the throat, they say, "Plunge
Your feet in freezing water"; but if it's a crust
That's stuck there, the remedy is bread from the same loaf
Rammed into both ears. Headaches
Are best cured, they claim, by pouring vinegar
Over door hinges, and applying the resultant sludge
To the temples. They venerate the mole, and trust
The entrails of no creature as they trust
Those of this tiny blind tunneler through the bowels
Of the earth. Anyone who consumes a mole's heart, fresh
And still beating, will see like a prophet
Into the future. Avoid
Using a vulture's feather as a toothpick; for sweet breath
Rub the ashes of burnt mice mixed with honey
Around the gums, then clean
With a porcupine quill. Should you suffer
From persistent pain in the abdomen, tear open
A bat . . .

      . . . beyond
Stretches a desert where flickering ghosts crowd
Round the startled traveler, then vanish. Nature
Would have us wonder
At her ingenuity, and creates men who never spit,
Who stand all day watching the burning sun journey across the sky,
    moving
Only to shift their weight from foot
To foot. Some are born with two pupils
In one eye, and in the other, if you look
Closely, you will see the image of a horse. There are regions

Where no shadows
Ever fall, where men sleep but do not dream, where human
Skulls serve as water vessels. Those on whose mouths
A swarm of bees settled when they were young, will sway
Whole peoples with their clear
Golden words in later life. But no
Words spoken of any kind, in any tongue, can allay
The griefs of aging, or deny our racked bodies their final, sweet
Release into oblivion: sure signs
Of impending death include numbness, raucous laughter, mottled
Eyes or nostrils, fingers toying obsessively with the tasseled
Fringe of the bedspread . . .

The Münster Anabaptists

The scribes
of Strasbourg gazed in wonder
at the soaring tower; inside was a cage
in which the itinerant preacher
Melchior Hoffman
was imprisoned, his wanderings
over; "Woe," wailed
Melchior Hoffman, night and day, hour
after hour, rattling the iron bars
of his cage, "Woe
will engulf you, *you,* O damned
and sinning scribes of Strasbourg."

II

We saw it—a cloud in the shape of an angry bishop
Looming over us, dwarfing us; and we gasped as a blade
Of lightning tore apart the cloud, and it dissolved as the sun set.

So we drove the unclean from Münster, laughing
As they fled, unbaptised and naked, into knifing winds
And frenzied snow; and Jan Matthys, our bony prophet, was content.

And he decreed all money, and all silver and gold, be surrendered, and all
Legal deeds, and books, save the Bible, be burned; for the Kingdom
Of God was at hand, and doubters, like this querulous blacksmith, must die.

And some sang a hymn, and praised gaunt, fiery Jan Matthys, the Lord's
Anointed, once a baker in Haarlem, while some crawled
On their knees across the marketplace, imploring forgiveness.

And daily the hirelings besieging us were touched by the Lord, and laid down
Their arms, and were admitted to Münster; and in Münster they heard
Jan Matthys declare the siege, and the world, would end this Easter.

Encased in armor, lo! our own Gideon rides forth through the city gates
Leading his tiny band of chosen followers; and we, from the walls of Münster, watch
The bishop's Landsknechte quail, and brace themselves for slaughter.

III

Dithering

"Let spades be trumps!" she said, and trumps they were; it leaves
us free to cry, and whisper to their souls to
go. Nor wilt thou
then forget where are the legs with which
you run, Hurroo! Hurroo!, or wake
and feel the fell of dark. Like an angel came
I down,
when my dream was near the moon,
the crux left of the watershed, and the stars that usher
evening rose. He
is not here; but far away—o'er Bodley's dome his future labors
spread. "Have you been
out?" "No." "And don't want to, perhaps?" Men shut their doors
against a setting sun, and high
the mountaintops, in cloudy air, and instantly the whole
sky burned with fury against them. They
like to drink beer, and each one had
a little wicker basket, made of fine twigs, entrailed curiously:
patient, look, thou watchest the last oozings hours by hours,
etherized
upon a midnight dreary, where no flower can wither; many
a spring I shoot up fair, the book on the writing
table, the hand in the breast pocket.

Rinse and Repeat

The Zabbaleen left drought-stricken rural Egypt for Cairo in the 1950s.
Our unique formula helps condition and smooth damaged hair.

They brought their pigs, which they fed with the city's discarded scraps and peelings.
Drench with water, then massage deeply into scalp and roots.

Soon the Zabbaleen had evolved into a vast, informal garbage team.
There's more to life than hair, but it's a good place to start.

Young Zabbaleen scavengers attend a school called "Spirit of Youth."
Rich in essential oils—take a deep breath and enjoy the delicious smell.

"Spirit of Youth" is sponsored by a manufacturer of bottles of shampoo.
Boost and volumize lifeless hair by removing dirt and debris that weigh hair down.

Sorting and studying empty bottles of shampoo, young Zabbaleen learn to read and
        write.
Avoid contact with eyes—should this occur rinse immediately with clean, warm
        water.

Decree Nisi

On this crescent beach, sorrow; tell me
About it, digger
Of cockles and clams.

* * *

Wearing new aviator
Ray-Bans at night, I see myself
In grainy miniature: trigger-happy, falling.

* * *

The last weekend in May; Broadstairs'
Moonlit arcades, and cormorants'
Cries stretched across the water.

* * *

As the octopus dreams
In the octopus pot, I gather leaves and grass
And feathers to throw at shadows, silhouettes.

Masse und Macht

One Inch
of Emotion, One Inch
of Ash, I read, in fiery letters, on a skin-
tight T-shirt
passing, a little too close, at rush hour, under the soaring stanchions
of Hungerford Bridge. Some
reflex that verged
on a shiver
set me thinking of Elias
Canetti, and how he claimed that we hate
to be touched, however
gently, in a slow-moving crowd, and so
apologize profusely when we brush
against a stranger. Looming

looming up through
the haze, Charing Cross, its maw
agape, its tentacles twitching
and probing. A busker, cross-
legged, hunched beneath the balustrade, was merrily tooting "The Bard
of Armagh" into a child's
pink, see-through recorder—occasionally
plucking it from his lips
so he could sing
in a reedy voice: "And when Sergeant Death
in his cold arms shall embrace me, oh lull me to sleep
with sweet Erin Go Bragh . . ." Beyond

and beneath swirled
the Thames, at once

murky and aflame. I watched,
blinking, the setting sun
catch and burnish the glass and flanks of the cabs
and buses, the opaque 4x4s
and low-roofed cars and sleek
tourist coaches
crawling across Waterloo Bridge; an almost
empty inbound commuter train clanked slowly
by . . . In the lull that ensued, the merry busker's tooting grew
hauntingly erratic, then died
away, and with a dip
of the shoulder I surged on, through a swarm of chattering
language students, all carrying light-blue knapsacks, and filling
the air with the strains of their dear

native land.

Wooster and Jeeves

"It was to the English colonist like a revolt of the domestic staff. . . . It was as though Jeeves had taken to the jungle." —Graham Greene, *Ways of Escape*

Malaria, sleeping sickness, bilharzia, yellow fever—Wooster
had seen them all afflict his faithful Jeeves;
now a new disease was rife among the Kikuyu,
carried not by mosquitoes or tsetse flies, but on the tip of a simi or panga.
The shrieking of baboons seemed deafening as he stepped
onto the veranda, and scanned the horizon, muttering a mild oath.

Even his own docile houseboy had succumbed, he suspected, and taken the vile oath,
had lapped up a gourd of goat's blood (Bertie Wooster
shuddered at the thought) then stuck a thorn seven times into the goat's eyeball.
      Under the steps
to an outhouse he'd found bloodstained banana leaves. Summoned, Jeeves
just shook his head, and murmured, "Mau Mau . . . panga . . .
Bwana beware . . ." Beneath, coiled like a snake, was an animal intestine the Kikuyu

believed had magical powers . . . closing his eyes, Bertie recalled the first Kikuyu
he'd hired, and the private oath
to treat them kindly that he'd made; their pangas
caught the sun, and flamed when they moved. The rich red soil of Wooster
Farm was perfect for sisal and maize; he set to work some fifty Jeeves
to clear the bush, and plough the land, and together, step by step

they battled the wilderness . . . Abruptly, dusk fell. Shrouded figures were stepping
out of the Aberdare forest, heading for an isolated homestead or Kikuyu
collaborator. Their leader, Colonel Jeeves,

whistled like a bird, and his men advanced. Tonight an oath-
breaking traitor, or maybe a Wooster
would wake to an unfamiliar noise, and moonlight on a falling panga.

"Is this," the British Club's leading man demanded, clutching the air, "a panga
which I see before me, the handle toward my hand?" Steps
on the gravel prated softly of watchmen guarding young Woosters—
that, or the approach of murder most foul. The Kikuyu
rebel must be unseamed from the nave to the chops, the hateful oath
retracted, and poor deluded Jeeves

restored to his senses. It was decreed, therefore, that any Jeeves
or witchdoctor caught killing a sheep or a goat with a panga
in order to administer a Mau Mau oath
of allegiance, must die. The guilty mounted the steps
to makeshift gallows, commending their souls to their Kikuyu
Ngai. The last thing they saw was the razor wire of Camp Wooster.

One morning Bertie Wooster was studying the newspaper. Many Jeeves
had come and gone. But was this dead Kikuyu, his panga
by his side, the one who'd stopped him stepping on a cobra? Yes, it *was* him, he'd
    take an oath!

Released

to wander
between the winds, and find
no home, to scour
the thickets for hips, frail
wisps
of animal fur or fluff, picnic
detritus, water
as it trickles between rustling
ferns or oozing, densely
wadded layers
of leaves . . .

ka-
boom ka-boom, the heart
pounds, while
blood as red as holly berries
stains the shepherd's purse on which
he wakes. The far-
off murmur
of waves breaking
on shingle throbs
and burns in his fevered
eardrums; following
his own
scarlet trail through campion and saxifrage and sweet
cicely, he stumbles
downhill, from trampled
copse to ravaged clearing, a cloud

of flies
about his groin. Curious
gulls wheel, shrieking, around the lip
of the cliff
he finally reaches, above an empty, iron-
gray sea.

"My mind,"
he wails, "has grown
keen as the razor-
edged steel I pressed
against, and then into, and through my soft, secret
flesh . . . oh years, how was it
you led to this? I, the acknowledged
flower of the gymnasium, my lintels decked
each sunrise with orchids, am now
self-plucked, doomed to prowl
these barren, savage tracts, forever, and serve . . ."

The dread
Cybele has heard
enough: unleashing
the left-hand lion
from her chariot's traces, she lowers
her pale mouth
to his pricked and tawny ear, and whispers, "Go,
ferocious one, go, and scare
this lily-
livered acolyte, so that never
again will he dream of straying

from the groves and streams sacred
to my law. Lash
yourself forward with your swingeing tail, until I can feel
the land tremble
under your thundering paws." The yoke
pin lifted, he bounds
in a rabid frenzy toward the hapless,
grieving Attis. As the lion
springs, Attis screams
to Cybele, begs
Cybele, his tormentor, his goddess, for help.

Decree Absolute

                                    . . . pink-
veined blossoms falling, the face, lightly
tattooed, of a god
carved, frowning,
into the bole
of a lime tree . . . *tchack-tchack tsk*
tchack-tchack
tsk laments
a fidgety stonechat, inflating
his rusty breast, his wings and tail
a blur; one
restless, beady eye
fastens on a tiny, green-shelled snail gliding
over a shadowy patch of roots
and drifted petals
and moss.

The Confidence Man

I dreamt some children I'd never met were playing at being Hölderlin walking to Bordeaux. One carried a bulging canvas knapsack on his back, and was wearing knee breeches, a collarless jacket, a three-cornered hat, and a pair of stout leather boots; his clothes were powdered white with the dust of the road. Another periodically shook his fist at the flawless skies, and cried out *Susette! Susette! oh my Susette!* whenever he stumbled, or paused to rest. The third, a flaxen-haired girl, floated some distance in front; dressed in gingham, she advanced swiftly, but seemed to move neither her legs nor her arms, which dangled limply at her sides; over her head hung a searing white halo.

*   *   *

I sat
in the dark ivy, listening. These
fibrous networks
of arteries
and nerves are to alter
the way air itself enters
and leaves
the lungs. Through me
the voices of plover, of the ousel, of curlew, of buzzard
and snipe; and with this
fingernail
I flicked a pair of glittering ladybirds
as they mated on the curled leaf
of an apple tree, in May.

Fragments

When dawn, wearing golden sandals, awoke me,
I began to crawl, burning, shivering, to my uncurtained window;
Migrating birds streamed over the dark sea.

Who can quench the ingenious fires of cruelty?
I was dreaming of white-fetlocked horses conferring in a meadow
When dawn, wearing golden sandals, awoke me.

On my stopped loom, a sort of landscape: icy
Peaks, serrated as daggers; a corpse, and beside it a crow,
And migrating birds streaming over the dark sea.

Fat, autumnal flies alight on my sheets, rainbow-hued, dizzy;
This one on my wrist—its mandibles quiver, its gibbous eyes glow . . .
Then dawn, wearing golden sandals, awoke me.

Merciless daughter of Zeus, immortal Aphrodite,
Come to me, sing to me, low-voiced, in sorrow
Of migrating birds that stream over the dark sea.

Cast aside your spangled headband; in my mirror I see
You beneath these stringy locks, puckered lips, and tearstained cheeks . . . go,
Migrating birds, stream over the dark sea;
And dawn, wearing golden sandals, awake me.

NEW POEMS

Dark Matter

The estuary mud
of the Thames, lit by the rage of a blood-
red sun, laid bare
the future: in the squelching ooze the river god
sculpted our city
in miniature, molding the heavy silt
until rooftop and turret and arch lay spread
before us, exact
and glistening; then he swelled
with displeasure, and swept it away
in a swirl
of sediment . . .

                    * * *

Dark
matter
that I guessed
was originally jam
came to encrust whatever books he begged, or borrowed
or stole. Some
got scribbled in, and some
illuminated: I trace
like a scar the spindly outline of a figure
dwarfed by a collapsing tower
sketched on the title page of *Brideshead
Revisited* . . .

                    * * *

On loan
to a new media outfit, and holed up
for a week or so in a shivering
hotel in beseiged
Aleppo, all communications
down, and the road to Damascus one endless
roadblock, she plunged
both hands into an overflowing
rucksack, rummaged awhile, then hauled
out her, or his, or even my
black-
spined Tacitus . . .

Gaius Suetonius Paulinus

(after Tacitus)

Gaius Suetonius Paulinus
at that time
controlled Britain. According
to rumor, which loves to pit
one man against another, he had grown deeply envious
of Corbulo, and yearned to equal
his rival's recovery of Armenia
by himself gloriously putting to the sword
some foreign adversary. Therefore, fixing
on the isle of Anglesey, where many refugees
had sought safety, he had constructed an armada
of flat-bottomed boats, and these conveyed
his foot soldiers across the treacherous, shallow
sound. His cavalry had to ford
the cold waters on their mounts, and even,
in the deeper parts, to swim beside their horses.

Along the shore, near
the tideline, men
waited, bristling with weapons, and weaving
between them, women in funereal black
like Furies, hair
hanging down, brandishing torches. And Druids, everywhere
Druids, shrieking, hands lifted
to the heavens, stunning the invaders with their harrowing
curses . . . dismayed
and paralyzed, even the battle-hardened quailed, seemed

almost to offer up their bodies for slaughter; until,
roused by their general, and urging
themselves not to be daunted by a band
of fanatical women, they advanced
and attacked, decimating
all they encountered, slashing and burning, setting
alight the foe with the flames
of their own torches . . . Victory
accomplished, a garrison
was established and the island's
sacred groves razed: for those savages would drown
their altars in human blood and consult their gods by probing
the entrails of butchered prisoners. It was,
however, while he was busy
accomplishing all this, that Suetonius learned of a sudden
rebellion, of unspeakable
mayhem, of terror engulfing the skeleton
army he'd left to defend
the colony's main province.

Show Time

Tempus fugit every sundial
proclaims, yet over and over
time seems to swoon, or to expand, even
to grind
to a juddering halt
when I blog; a dreadful day
online, I think I mean, is a dreadful
day forever. My current
screensaver is a sniper's-
eye view of a traffic warden
leaning
back to photograph
an illegally parked car. Hatchet-
faced tax inspectors invade my dreams: "We need
you to live," they murmur
as they pass, lips
nearing, even brushing
my helpless ear.

           In what
wrinkle, in what furrow
or fissure lurks
the longing to make the worst
happen? As if
I had conjured them, one
Halloween two hooded figures loomed
above me
on a bridge I was dawdling across

in downtown Boston; their cradled
half bricks crashed
con brio, with energy and purpose
into my swirling
stream of thoughts . . . treats
for the favored few, endless
tricks for the others . . . traveling by water
is best because you n-n-n-n-never
have to go uphill . . .

                  I lay
prone awhile . . . then, springing
to life, into action,
I fled. Something—my heart—boomed
and echoed like pursuing
footsteps on asphalt. *Leeeeeft,* a voice shouted
in a comic French accent, *erpp yer aass.* Laughter.
Don't stop don't stop
till you get enough! "Are you," I recall
demanding of a friendly
paramedic as he shone his pencil torch
deep into my eyes, "an electric light bulb, and
if so,
what wattage?" No one
I met seemed to know
about soldier ants, about how
their jaws, or maybe their claws, are used in Africa
to stitch up wounds.

Discharged
with a warning, how quietly
I crept home through the mazy, moonlit
streets of Roxbury, avoiding
alleys and skips, my scars
stinging like unwisely
acquired tattoos. Halloween
was over. High
above rows of ghostly buildings
hollowed out
by descendants of the locust or the palmer-
or cankerworm, giant
Citgo and Exxon signs smiled
encouragement. Glancing
down, I noticed a red coin
of blood disfiguring
the left knee of my chinos—and thinking
this funny, I began to limp.

Streets II

(*after Verlaine*)

A river in the street!
Outlandish apparition—behind
A wall that's five feet high
Water flowing
In silence, opaque yet pure, flowing
Through the slumbering borough.

Sallow as a woman's
Corpse, the water streaming
Through this wide canal can hope
To reflect nothing but the fog; first
Dawn, meanwhile, illuminates the black
And amber houses it flows past.

(Paddington)

Unreal

        . . . I drank
and was surprised
to see what looked like tea leaves
at the bottom
of the cup . . . minutes
later a great warm green wave
or cloud
began advancing toward me. "Look at the boats
on his shirt," I felt myself trying
to say, in Spanish, or Moroccan, yet knowing
I knew
none of the words . . .

        it was bright
morning, and the train had arrived
and emptied
at Chamartín before I finally
pried open my eyes, and saw
on the carriage floor
nothing but an unfamiliar
pair of trainers: cracked
white leather, with three green stripes. "Mister—
or rather Herr—Adolf
Dassler made these," I thought. But which
of the two friendly men with whom
I'd shared the carriage, and some wine,
had been wearing them? I pondered
this awhile, then fell
asleep again . . .

and did
Herr Dassler visit, personally, all the cities inscribed
on his trainers? Koln, Dublin, Paris, Montreal,
Kopenhagen, Bern, Amsterdam . . . and fit
the trainer to the city? Rom, like these, Vienna,
London . . .

                    Señor Dassler, I am dreaming of you
on a bench on a platform in a train station
in Madrid, unable
to wake up, a pair
of your trainers, that weren't mine, but now are,
on my feet . . .

I am swimming, Herr
Dassler, in your wake, though I fear
you are dead, a corpse washed clean by the numbing tides
with three slanting stripes emblazoned
on your chest, your passport and your wallet
drifting to the ocean floor . . .

                    I discovered
in a pocket—oh! the kindness
of strangers!—about
forty pesetas; but casting
around for a joke or silver lining, I found
nada—or niente, as I put it
to my shoes . . . closing
my eyes, I imagined fingers untying
and easing off my Reeboks, as the train

hurtled through the darkness, the men trying
them on in turn, the ex-owner of these
flexing his toes, padding up and down, nodding
approval. They must have whispered
like parents, as they lifted my shirt and unfastened
my money belt, or perhaps, more like surgeons, they used
scissors, or a knife . . .

                       snicker-snack! I watched
the vorpal blade trace
arabesques across my breastbone, hover, then slide
between two ribs. *Chug-chug*
went the trains. The heat
was building, the potion
at last wearing off. How light
I'd be, I now
began to reason, as quick and canny
as a lizard, a perfectly camouflaged
lizard, who'd shed a skin and acquired a new
way of walking.

Adrift

Colonel Muammar Gaddafi's wife, or rather
widow, recently wrote to me asking for help in transferring
some important financial assets from a secret location: only I,
she insisted, had the expertise to perform this complex operation.

Is there a more ferocious texter than General Pinochet's
daughter? I've no idea how she got my number.
It seems that her fridge-freezer is empty, and her bedroom
bugged; now her toenails need clipping, now she can't find her keys.

A minor ex-mistress of Laurent Gbagbo's tweets practically
every day. He, apparently, has become a serious fan
of my poetry. She has a cache of uncut diamonds for sale, a terrible
headache most mornings, and a fear of flying in any class but first.

I'm just too tired to think of replying to this e-mail
inviting me to go trekking in the Himalayas with a distant "cousin"
of Pervez Musharraf. The gender of this "cousin" is unclear,
and I fear his—or her—"invitation" is really a threat.

"You have reached 0207 . . ." my machine was intoning
but I snatched the handset from the cradle; I'd urgent
business with a dude I'd just met—a cool cool
customer called Rafa something something something, then definitely

ending in Marcos.

In Loco Parentis

were some quite creepy men—one
used to lie down
on the dayroom floor, then get us all
to pile on top of him—and a basilisk-
eyed matron in a blue uniform with a watch
dangling
beneath her right
collarbone. *Thump thump*
thump went her footsteps, making
the asbestos ceiling tiles shiver, and me
want to hide, or run like a rabbit
in a fire . . .
            What we lost, we lost
forever. A minor
devil played at chess
with us, forcing
the pieces to levitate
and hover, flourishing swords, in midair. I'd grasp
them now, the orotund bishop, the stealthy
knight, the all-
knowing queen,
but they dissolve
in my fingers, refuse
to return to the board, to their squares.

Aloft

Trust me, or rather *text* me—I need
right now the winged
the divine
happiness of conception—*zhuuum* . . . recall
for me the lingering
aftershave of the one who hoisted
you high in the Country Club car park, and got sent
to jail for molesting
minors. Attach
a snap of the lonely peacock
of Holland Park, his beak
parted to scream, tail fan arced and quivering, dark
eye outraged . . . We turn
aside, then peer
inward, composed
of insurgent, or of waning
Eros, of inconvenient aches and pimples, of DNA-
inflected dust.

                    *   *   *

An airport
is a delightful retreat for any mind grown weary
of the struggles of life. The vast expanse of sky, the shifting
architecture of the clouds, the dizzying colors
of the tail fins,
the beacons flashing on the runway, all
create a prism which is marvelously calculated

to entertain but not weary
the eye.

I like to think of uniformed pilots in cockpits surveying
flickering banks of instruments, of planes shuddering
into motion, ordered this way
and that by air traffic controllers sipping lukewarm coffee
in towers.

Above all there is a mysterious, aristocratic sort of pleasure to be
derived, by those who have themselves lost all curiosity, all ambition,
and now lean on their elbows on the rail of the viewing deck, from
contemplating the arrivals and departures of those who still harbor
belief and purpose, who are still driven by the desire to travel, or by

the urge

to enrich themselves.

                    *   *   *

Where are—I mean what happened to—my Junior
Jet Club Logbook and my framed
certificates awarded for having flown
25,000 miles—50,000 miles—
75,000 miles—100,000 miles—
after which we gave up counting
or they ran out of certificates?

World Enough

Yo-ho! haul high the Jack, or the Jolly
R-R-Roger, however
tattered and torn, but also
r-r-remove a pirate's
favorite letter, turning
friend to *fiend,* and *fright*
to *fight*! The Empire
was flummoxed, and dissolving
fast when we
set sail on the Seven Seas, late, late
buccaneers in quest
of whatever booty
remained: a retinue
of "bearers," a bare-
footed gardener, lychees and lime juice and papaya
brought to us on the veranda, a chauffeur
in a crisp
white shirt with pleats and pockets
and epaulettes . . . my sister
wept when "David," an aging, impassive servant
dismissed for getting "filthy drunk"
on arak, returned, red-
eyed, to retrieve a cushion
he'd forgotten . . . I watched
him adjust
his bundle, rise, then stagger off again, his wispy
gray hair coming loose
from its bun . . . no more

142

dusting of ebony heads
from Nigeria, onyx elephants, sphinxes carved
out of soapstone; our gaudy, bug-eyed
demon masks, or the glass
protecting seven
saffron-robed Masai warriors leaning
on their spears in a clearing
at midnight; a moon-
landing souvenir mug, a slab
of agate on a Chinese chest, my pen-
holder made
from the hide
of a lion.

Under the Lime Trees

All that glitters
is not glass, but lots and lots
of it is, mused
the helmeted cyclist . . . O you fast-
spinning tires, so delicately ridged, so like the scales
of a young crocodile—avoid
whatever sparkles, and that
straggle-haired woman weaving
her way briskly against the traffic, her hands
a jiving blur as she belts
out snatches of *We're just*
two little girls from Little Rock . . . the one who broke
my heart . . .
in Little Rock . . . Are these
I spy the deserving
poor, fully adrift, or breast-fed bohemians (weird
thought of the day!) jostling on a street corner beside
an all but emptied rack
of Boris bikes? Wolves
living on wind, sur le Noël, morte
saison . . .
          we do not feel
the speck of dust that alights
on our shoulder, nor
its fatal cousin, the germ we inhale, unknowing,
and cannot spit out. It slides
through the unmapped city
within. Responsive

cells divide or move, suddenly
restless, alert, driving, dragging
from the abyss an image
of myself cowboy-hatted, aged three, proudly astride
an East African zebra. The spongy marrow
buried in our bones
enriches the blood that unites, as it flows, nerve
and muscle, tissue and tendon, propelling
all smoothly forward like a river swirling
over its unseen bed; while every
active capillary, if challenged, or opposed, or howsoever
aroused, dilates
in bold defiance, in outright
scorn of the cold footsteps creeping like mist . . .

                                          blink,
and click your heels one-two-three, and the yellow
brick road is thigh-
deep in nettles and willowherb. Even
when it's invisible the sun
flings into space its gassy flames, each day
enthrones itself, and we, too, must purge our minds of the inert
and confining, dwell
in thoughts that breathe, and words that burn, or shine
brightly as a falling
guillotine . . . blink
again and the fantastical
flow of money
and data bursts like a blood vessel, scattering
the crowds gathered beneath the weeping
limes. It happened

I fell in with one kicking wildly
at piles of sticky, heart-shaped leaves—his cheeks were furrowed
with scars, and his left ear seemed torn: "Follow,"
he confided, "the scent to the vixens' lair . . . take up
your broken bicycle, and with both hands hurl it as far . . . as far . . ."

Notes

"Stop knocking . . ." is a version of "Ne hurtez plus à l'uis de ma Pensée" by Charles d'Orléans.

"The Casket" is based on an episode in Book VI of the *Metamorphoses* by Apuleius.

"The Death of Petronius" is adapted from a passage in Book 16 of *Annales* by Tacitus.

"White Nights" is adapted from various passages in *De Rerum Natura* by Lucretius.

Part 2 of "Hourglass" is adapted from a section of *De Consolatione Philosophiae* by Boethius, and Part 3 from a work by Matsuo Bashō called *Nozarashi kikō,* a title variously translated as *Journal of Bleached Bones in a Field, Travelogue of Weather-Beaten Bones,* and *The Records of a Weather-Exposed Skeleton.*

"Ravished" is an elegy for the poet Mick Imlah (1956–2009).

Parts of "A Natural History" are adapted from various passages of *Naturalis Historia* by Pliny the Elder.

"Dithering" is a cento inspired by the opening lines of T. S. Eliot's "The Love Song of J. Alfred Prufrock."

"Released" is based on the story of Attis in Catullus LXIII.

"Fragments" makes use of a number of images from the poetry of Sappho.

"Gaius Suetonius Paulinus" is adapted from a passage in Book 14 of *Annales* by Tacitus.

"Aloft" makes use of the prose poem "Le Port" by Charles Baudelaire.

Colophon

Selected Poems was designed at Coffee House Press,
in the historic Grain Belt Brewery's Bottling House
near downtown Minneapolis. The text is set in Garamond.

Coffee House Press

The mission of Coffee House Press is to publish exciting, vital, and enduring authors of our time; to delight and inspire readers; to contribute to the cultural life of our community; and to enrich our literary heritage. By building on the best traditions of publishing and the book arts, we produce books that celebrate imagination, innovation in the craft of writing, and the many authentic voices of the American experience.

Visit us at coffeehousepress.org.

Funder Acknowledgments

Coffee House Press is an independent, nonprofit literary publisher. Our books are made possible through the generous support of grants and gifts from many foundations, corporate giving programs, state and federal support, and through donations from individuals who believe in the transformational power of literature. Coffee House Press receives major operating support from Amazon, the Bush Foundation, the Jerome Foundation, the McKnight Foundation, from the National Endowment for the Arts—a federal agency, from Target, and in part from a grant provided by the Minnesota State Arts Board through an appropriation by the Minnesota State Legislature from the State's general fund and its arts and cultural heritage fund with money from the vote of the people of Minnesota on November 4, 2008, and a grant from the Wells Fargo Foundation of Minnesota. Coffee House also receives support from: several anonymous donors; Suzanne Allen; Elmer L. and Eleanor J. Andersen Foundation; Mary & David Anderson Family Foundation; Around Town Agency; Patricia Beithon; Bill Berkson; the E. Thomas Binger and Rebecca Rand Fund of the Minneapolis Foundation; the Patrick and Aimee Butler Family Foundation; The Buuck Family Foundation; Claire Casey; Ruth Dayton; Dorsey & Whitney, LLP; Mary Ebert and Paul Stembler; Chris Fischbach and Katie Dublinski; Fredrikson & Byron, P.A.; Katharine Freeman; Sally French; Anselm Hollo and Jane Dalrymple-Hollo; Jeffrey Hom; Carl and Heidi Horsch; Kenneth Kahn; Alex and Ada Katz; Stephen and Isabel Keating; the Kenneth Koch Literary Estate; Kathy and Dean Koutsky; the Lenfestey Family Foundation; Carol and Aaron Mack; George Mack; Gillian McCain; Mary McDermid; Sjur Midness and Briar Andresen; the Nash Foundation; Peter & Jennifer Nelson; the Rehael Fund of the Minneapolis Foundation; Schwegman, Lundberg & Woessner, P.A.; Kiki Smith; Jeffrey Sugerman and Sarah Schultz; Patricia Tilton; the Archie D. & Bertha H. Walker Foundation; Stu Wilson and Mel Barker; the Woessner Freeman Family Foundation; Margaret and Angus Wurtele; and many other generous individual donors.

To you and our many readers across the country,
we send our thanks for your continuing support.

NEW POETRY FROM
COFFEE HOUSE PRESS

Psychedelic Norway by John Colburn
978-1-56689-335-0
"John Colburn does here for poetry
what George Saunders has done for
the short story." —DOBBY GIBSON

Dance by Lightsey Darst
978-1-56689-334-3
"*DANCE* is to *The Divine Comedy* as Darst is
to Dante: heretical." —BRIAN TEARE

Collected Poems by Ron Padgett
978-1-56689-342-8
"Ron Padgett makes the most quiet and
sensible of feelings a provocatively
persistent wonder." —ROBERT CREELEY

Bleed Through by Michael Davidson
978-1-56689-339-8
"*Bleed Through* is a book we have
needed for a very long time. What a joy
to have it in hand." —RON SILLIMAN

Dark. Sweet. by Linda Hogan
978-1-56689-351-0
"These poems in particular cross over to
speak for us in the shining world. They
bring back words for healing, the distilled
truth of all these stories that are killing us
with tears and laughter." —JOY HARJO

MARK FORD was born in Nairobi, Kenya. He has published three collections of poetry, and a biography of the French writer Raymond Roussel. He has also translated Roussel's *New Impressions of Africa,* and is the editor of *London: A History in Verse.* He lives in London.